The Teacher,
The Twin, &
The Tower

The Gospel of Thomas along with the Gospel of Mary:
Modern Translations with Parallel Comparisons,
Commentaries, and Contemplative Companion

First edition

3

Preface

The book in front of you updates, expands (more about this in a bit) and combines the complete *Thom's Gospel* and *Maggie's Gospel* with their parallel comparison translations and commentaries previously released. It speaks to what many scholars believe is among the earliest of Jesus' teachings. This is the Gospel According to Thomas and the Gospel of Mary Magdalene, rendered plain and simply.

If you've picked this book up, I would guess you've at least heard about the Gospel of Thomas. You may have read some of its sayings before. For that matter, what you've read in it might even seem quite familiar since 72 of its 114 Sayings (these are like verses, sometimes called "logion") are similar in the canonical gospels, and 34 coincide with John's Gospel.

The Gospel of Thomas (or The Gospel According to Thomas) is unlike the other gospels, in that it is a collection of sayings and dialogues of Jesus, referenced in early writings but lost for about 1500 years. In 1897 and 1903, Greek fragments were found in Egypt at Oxyrhynchus and in 1945, a couple of copies were found at Nag Hammadi.

We know of its widespread use throughout Egypt, Rome, Greece, Syria, Persia, and South Asia. As well, we know it had favor with several early Christian communities, including the Desert Fathers, the Naassenes, and with Encratites, Manichaeans, Valentinians, and others who grew in numbers for centuries. Clement and Origen even used it in written sermons that we still have. Sadly, many of the bishops then were trying to climb the religious ladder and wanted to distance themselves from anything that the proto-orthodox leaders didn't like, and heresy hunting was trending hard.

The Gospel of Mary Magdalene is less well known, but did get a boost from Dan Brown's novel, *The Da Vinci Code*. Of the various sources we have—from Oxyrhynchus, Akhmim, and Rylands Papyri—none are complete, having several pages missing, but the three surviving copies do point to a widespread familiarity within early Christian communities as well.

The Gospel of Mary continued to be read and appreciated in various communities. Stories of Mary Magdalene flourished throughout the Middle Ages and in legendary texts. Her gospel (a bit over half is all that remains) is mostly dialogue between Jesus, herself, and the other disciples.

What is presented today as the canonical New Testament is the result of Christianities (yes, there were several distinct "flavors") going from oppressed and persecuted to becoming a tool for political favor and dominance. The prevalence of several early gospels (at least 34 of them) and Christian writings became increasingly scarce. Many were purged by complicit leaders who were tasked to harmonize the message and ensure it aligned with the more posturing and domination-driven philosophical and theological schools during this time. Differences became demonized and thus, a number of the other gospels and foundational writings were destroyed.

Fortunately, a few were preserved by being hidden in places like Oxyrhynchus and Nag Hammadi, Akhmim, Al Minya, Qumran, Sinai, Xi'an, and so forth.

The Gospel of Thomas is unique in how it allows us to jump right into the teachings of Jesus apart from narration with supplementary stories that make Jesus a caricature. And the fragments we have of the Gospel of Mary seem to tie in well with where the Gospel of Thomas ends.

The Real "Problem" with Biblical Texts

There is something else we must consider that often goes overlooked. Our presumptions go unquestioned, unexamined, and we tend to project the Bible and whatever current Christian doctrines we have onto what we read and how we interpret these extra-canonical texts.

Most people don't realize that we also do this within the Bible itself with blending of gospels, epistles of Paul and doctrinal statements, not to mention with the harmonized accounts throughout antiquity and the Middle Ages.

Like stories about Jesus, those of Mary Magdalene have often been exaggerated, extrapolated and conflated, too. If we separate the accounts, and pull out the weeds that were sown in, we're left with a formidable figure who rightly inspires and exemplifies awe and wonder. She's a woman who is not only prominently mentioned in the Gospels   of

Matthew, Mark, Luke, and John, but in the Gospels of Thomas and Philip, too, not to mention her own (and the only woman to do so). And it doesn't end there. Aside from being in all four New Testament Gospels, we also find her in several early extra-canonical texts such as *Pistis Sophia*, *Dialogue of the Savior*, *Sophia of Jesus Christ*, *First Apocalypse of James*, *Acts of Philip*, and the *Manichaean Psalm Book*.

The important thing to remember is how vitally important it is to read each of these texts as they stand on their own. The canon (or collection of writings) was originally fluid for the first four and a half centuries, and in several cases much longer. Otherwise, we are stuck with this drastically homogenized, overdeveloped, dualistic image of Jesus that ends up coloring our understanding of what he taught and the different perspectives his earliest followers had.

How We Can Solve the Issue

So exactly how do we integrate these texts like the Gospel of Thomas and Gospel of Mary in our generation, 2000 years down the road, without the presumptions that we're trying to avoid? This is where I want to invite you into an experiment of sorts, to separate them from the overly familiar images of Jesus we have heard our whole lives and from the dogma we've created around him. We've made the very name of Jesus into a sacred cow, but in its day Ἰησοῦς was just another common name.

If we can let go of our initial preconceptions, I believe we can put ourselves more easily in the place of the first readers and have a better sense of context for these beautiful texts.

To help with this, we must let go of loaded words like *Kingdom, disciples, Father*, and so on. Specific names and attributions have been altered here as a means to dissociate projections from the original text.

Instead of reading about Jesus, you'll find a no-named *Teacher*. Gender doesn't matter, either. What this also does is allow space for you and me to recognize the fullness of the characters. As well, we have Thomas whose name means the *Twin*, and Mary Magdalene—of which "Magdala" means *Tower*—and we'll let their meanings stand in for their names.

There are several other familiar words we use to describe aspects in Christianity such as "Son of God," "Gospel," "ascension" and others. These terms were usurped by authors of the New Testament from Roman texts referring to the divinity of their emperors and the "good news" this brings. This was how their audience of the oral tradition and readers at the time would have understood it.

In this rendering, it's the *Teacher* who uses particular words in ways which challenge his audience's expectations just as Jesus would have done. When one sees words like "Kingdom," even though there were those in antiquity who were expecting that or wanting Jesus to take that role, that wasn't his message. To get to this, we must begin to drift away from the direction of a conquering and colonial sense

Sometimes Kingdom is also thought of as "heaven," but Jesus used the word to mean something other than a physical realm, although not an extra-dimensional location somewhere out there either. Kingdom for him was more of a space of Presence, Consciousness, or Unified Field. It's a place of shared responsibility and care, in awe and wonder of all that is, of the Ultimate Reality. It's one which includes all invisible and visible existence. Closer terms could be *Awareness, Source,* or *Oneness.*

When Jesus used the word "Father" for God, too, it would not have been familiar to his students and the crowds around him. It would've grabbed one's attention there.

What we hear from Jesus is a "Father" who created us into Being, even before we were birthed. It conveys (beyond *birther*) an intimacy and sharing of *spiritual DNA*. So, we should really switch "Father" out, as well. Jesus used it in a bit of a subversive sense, saying he (and we) come directly from the Ground of Being, Creator of the Universe, seen and unseen. It's in contrast to—as he also points out from time to time—any emphasis on genealogy or ethnicity.

It's worth noting that I am not trying to suggest one should abandon the Christian faith or anything when I substitute these terms. The method I'm using is meant to allow for a conversation of sorts between what we believe and what we are reading. As John Dominic Crossan aptly points out in the *Handbook for the Study of the Historical Jesus*, "*Narcissism* is an illusion claiming to see the past while only seeing the reflected present. *Positivism* is a delusion claiming to see the past without any interference from its own viewing eyes. *Interactivism* is our destiny."

So. if you're one that finds the *non-dual* syntax unusual, that's great! Consider the context of how provocative Jesus was being, too, in his time. You're in wonderful company!

I have used the earliest sources of these texts, in Coptic and Greek, to translate word for word to construct this transposition (a translation that takes context into account), and as such, I will take liberties here and there to subtly point out where the lines from these texts tie together. My focus is the cultural context of concepts that need clarifying, so we can understand how it might be seen today.

Seeing & Listening Beyond Eyes & Ears

What the *Teacher* wants is for us to listen carefully, from the heart, before moving to the head. As Meister Eckhart puts it, "God expects but one thing of you, and that is that you should come out of yourself in so far as you are a created being made and let God be God in you." It's often *we* who get in the way, and this is exactly what Jesus comes back to again and again in these gospels. We, too, must empty our cup of preconceptions to get a true taste of what he's saying here.

The Gospel of Thomas and the Gospel of Mary suspend themselves in perfect balance, fully supporting in one sense a (differentiated) social solidarity while also embracing Divine Union as a Singularity. Its pulse is undeniably close to the heart of the experiences, understandings and writings of the Christian mystics.

It should be noted that this book draws from a variety of sacred texts and ancient traditions as well as insights from recent writers. The content here is just my own interpreted understanding, along with the hope to help make all of it more accessible. I've included a list of references at the back should anyone wish to continue the experiment, and I encourage any readers—in the spirit of the Gospel of Thomas and our "journey of seeking and finding"—to explore these brilliant reflections from the writers in the bibliography more deeply.

How to Read This Book

Each chapter is broken down into bite-sized chunks of the modern translation, along with a comparative standard translation (by Mark M. Mattison from the public domain), the commentary that explains the choices made in translating it, and a contemplative companion that asks questions about the section, reflections to chew on at the time. Feel free to take some time and let the sayings stir up your own questions, too. (Seek and wonder, right?)

By luck, or divine providence, it works out to 40 sections. I mean, I feel like we're in good company with the 40 days that Jesus took to go out in the wilderness during his spiritual awakening, right? Let us, too, wander forth and find ourselves in wonder, just like he said.

Now it's time to taste how these *non-dual* notes from the Gospel of Thomas pair so well with those *mystical* flavors in Mary's. Consider taking one chapter per day. Let it sit on your spiritual tongue for a bit before swallowing. Then, let it digest and metabolize into energy for your soul throughout the day. And repeat.

If Thomas is all about "What is Reality and how to find it," then Mary is all about "the Nature of Reality and how to apply it." Delish!

I hope it speaks to you and encourages you along your journey. ~ *Toto*

THOM'S GOSPEL

These are some of the deeper things
that the Teacher shared while alive.
A student, the Twin, wrote them down.

Chapter 1 (Sayings 1 -3)
The True Self and Oneness

1

"The one who truly gets a hold of what these teachings mean will not taste of the true death."

2

"You're searching for something more. I get it. We long for belonging, for home, for wholeness, and for what's truly Real. In our journey of seeking and finding, we come across troubles, stuff that disrupts our plans and expectations, but then there will be these new perceptions that will amaze us and fill us with wonder. What the true seeker discovers is Oneness, being connected with the Source. Then we will sit with it in wholeness and Stillness, no longer unsettled, but in complete control."

3

"If someone tries to persuade you by saying, 'Look up to heaven! That's where God lives!', you know the birds are going to beat them to it. If they tell you, 'Ah Enlightenment; it's way out there, far beyond, to the other shore,' then fish will get there first. Instead, Ultimate Reality is right here, *both* within you and everywhere around you.

"Once you honestly realize your True Self, you'll understand that you are a Living Manifestation of the Living Source. However, if you don't know your True Self, then this very existence is meaningless."

(Standard translation: Saying 1
And he said, "Whoever discovers the meaning of these sayings won't taste death."

Saying 2

Jesus said, "Whoever seeks shouldn't stop until they find. When they find, they'll be disturbed. When they're disturbed, they'll be... amazed, and reign over the All."

Saying 3

Jesus said, "If your leaders tell you, 'Look, the kingdom is in heaven,' then the birds of heaven will precede you. If they tell you, 'It's in the sea,' then the fish will precede you. Rather, the kingdom is within you and outside of you.

"When you know yourselves, then you'll be known, and you'll realize that you're the children of the living Father. But if you don't know yourselves, then you live in poverty, and you are the poverty.")

What This Means

The prologue, or Saying #0, is like the part before chapter one—it's not the actual story, but it's there to introduce it and point to its start. In standard translations, the Gospel of Thomas text includes the author's name Didymos (Greek meaning "twin"), Judas (also Greek, meaning "praised"), and Thomas (Aramaic, also meaning "twin").

Sometimes the Gospel of Thomas seems confusing right from the *get-go* and becomes misunderstood right at the beginning. In standard translations, they say "These are the hidden teachings or secret teachings, as if they are some kind of esoteric teaching. Since the text was discovered in what was considered a collection of several gnostic and hermetic manuscripts, drawing lines to connect the various texts together, but it might be doing this where dots don't really connect. There's plenty of debate among recent scholars that range widely from monks to purveyors and traders to various groups trying to preserve them under threats of wiping them from Christian history. These are all theories.

There is little doubt that some early followers were said to have claimed to know secrets no one else knew. These gnostic-type communities appeared to like and to use the Gospel of Thomas. As mentioned in the preface, this was likely a reason why some early bishops and leaders steered away from "gnosticism," not wanting any association with what was being portrayed as heresy, which had become by now "wrong and evil" instead of just a difference of view. It was a time of struggle for pre-orthodox control. But correlation is not causation, and the manuscript itself does not have many of the key markings we find in what is considered Gnostic or demiurgical theology.

The word "hidden" used in the prologue, however, might simply point to something that is obscured in some way or not so obvious. It leads directly into deeper introspection into the *teaching* (not the hidden meaning). The Gospel of Thomas talks about this later (in Sayings 5 & 6, if you're the skip-ahead type.)

Here, *the Teacher* is reaching out to an audience who feels drawn to spiritual matters, or at least realizes there's got to be something more. How their journey may look is then explained. *Yeah, it's gonna get bumpy, but you're not gonna be able to shake its magnetic pull. And then a shift takes place which changes how you perceive Reality. It's here that you find peace, find rest, and discover your purpose for being alive.*

The Teacher goes on to tell us that others will try to explain how God is over here or over there, that enlightenment comes from doing this or that. Wherever it is or however you receive it, they view it as something that's outside of ourselves. But it's not. The Divine penetrates us, it infuses with us, and with everything, everywhere, material and immaterial, all at once. The Divine experiences Itself in Unity and Oneness with all of creation, which we can also experience and behold.

Swami Vivekananda used to say, "Don't (merely) seek God, just see Him (/Her)." Unless we behold Reality, what meaning, what purpose, and what value do we possibly have?

And how are we told we can approach this? We wonder. Wonder is a bridge that connects the head and heart.

We think all this matter and material is an ignorance or illusion that we must transcend, but that's not what *the Teacher* is saying, is it? The recognition that we are the "Living Manifestation of the Living Source" means that Ultimate Reality is downloaded into this reality. The Divine is both imbued and embodied in you and me and all this-ness. It is available right here, and *the Teacher* is clearly pointing it out how we are, as how Swami Sarvapriyananda refers to it, "dealing in cash, not credit."

Contemplative Reflection

What does it mean to truly "get a hold" of the teachings and to "not taste of the true death"?

This question prompts our reflection on the deeper meaning of the Teacher's words and the nature of spiritual understanding. It invites contemplation on the relationship between knowledge, awareness, and the experience of death (and even rebirth).

How can we reconcile the idea that the Ultimate Reality (or Kingdom of Heaven) is both within us and everywhere around us?

This question encourages exploration of the concept of non-duality and the interconnectedness of all things. It challenges us to consider how our inner experience of the Divine relates to the world we perceive around us.

Chapter 2 (Sayings 4 - 6)
Unlearning and Awakening

4

"A wise, old person won't hesitate to tell a newborn not to get in a rush, but instead to unbecome who they've been taught to believe they are and live their life fully. The seemingly first ones are the last to fully understand it, and yet they both become the Singularity."

5

"Try to recognize what is right in front of your face. All that is hidden from your perception will then be revealed. Right now, there's nothing obscured which is not close to being realized. Those who are still sleeping will be awakened soon enough."

6

The students asked, "Do you want us to do a fast? Is there a certain way we should pray?

How much should we donate to charity? Is there any special diet we should follow?"

The Teacher said, "Why would you fake any of this, when you hate it all? Don't do that. Because in Awareness, everything is completely out in the open and clearly understood. Stop believing that there are secrets that can stay covered up."

> (Standard Translation: Saying 4
> Jesus said, "The older person won't hesitate to ask a little seven-day-old child about the place of life, and they'll live, because many who are first will be last, and they'll become one."
>
> Saying 5
> Jesus said, "Know what's in front of your face, and what's hidden from you will be revealed to you, because there's nothing hidden that won't be revealed."

Saying 6

His disciples said to him, "Do you want us to fast? And how should we pray? Should we make donations? And what food should we avoid?"

Jesus said, "Don't lie, and don't do what you hate, because everything is revealed in the sight of heaven; for there's nothing hidden that won't be revealed, and nothing covered up that will stay secret.")

What This Means

"The first shall be last and last shall be first." It's a familiar phrase, right? There's a metamorphosis to it that transforms our perception, especially in contrast to human ambition. It leads into the next part where *the Teacher* sets up the concept of what's hidden in plain sight. What's truly important is not necessarily what we think we see, hear, taste, touch, or smell with our five senses. We are encouraged to perceive everything in another way, hidden from our casual view. As one goes deeper into their spiritual journey, one will start to *know* their True Self—not who they were raised by others to be or manipulated by Ego. They will "see" things in a newer, truer way, that had been hidden from our perspective before.

The Teacher also addresses some of the problems with religiousness, especially the unnecessary expectations it demands and how it piles all this guilt on us. In turn, one makes demands on themselves, too.

It should be noted that in a couple of areas throughout the text, it sounds like *the Teacher* is bashing rituals and traditions. A better understanding of it is how easily one can become too prescriptive, how constricting and misdirecting rituals can be; too limiting and focused on the wrong things—surface stuff, without depth, value, or efficacy. The Path we're on does not need these gatekeepers and religious police over such matters. There's no insiders' advantage to be had.

Contemplative Reflection

How can we "unbecome" who we've been taught to believe we are? What does it mean to truly live life fully?

This question prompts reflection on the process of shedding societal conditioning and discovering our authentic selves. It encourages us to examine the ways in which external influences have shaped our beliefs and behaviors, and to consider what it might look like to live in alignment with our deepest truth.

What is the relationship between our own perceptions and reality? How can we cultivate that deeper awareness of "what is right in front of our face"?

This question invites contemplation on the nature of perception and the possibility of accessing a deeper level of reality. It challenges us (and what a challenge it is!) to question our assumptions and to explore practices that might help us see beyond the surface level of things.

Chapter 3 (Sayings 7 & 8)
Inner Essence and True Knowing

7

"Have you ever noticed how the natural world operates from this deep sense of freedom? Be like the hunter out in the wild, searching for their prey and taking it down, then devouring even this very understanding down to its bones—its essence.

"How truly heartbreaking it is wherever the illusion and the ego consume us, instead. We wind up believing *that* is who we are. It's ridiculous to think that merely being human gives us dominance over all of nature. This is simply not true."

8

"One could say that a person who knows their True Self is like a girl who loves to fish, putting her whole head and heart into it.

"She throws her nets out into the deep and pulls them up. It's loaded with small fish. But there, in the huge pile, one singular, large fish catches her eye. Of course, *she* easily knows exactly what to do. All the rest of the fish are tossed back into the deep waters. Only the great fish remains. This is worth understanding."

(Standard Translation: Saying 7
Jesus said, "Blessed is the lion that's eaten by a human and then becomes human, but how awful for the human who's eaten by a lion, and the lion becomes human."

Saying 8
He said, "The human being is like a wise fisher who cast a net into the sea and drew it up from the sea full of little fish. Among them the wise fisher found a fine large fish and cast all the little fish back down into the sea, easily choosing the large fish. Anyone who has ears to hear should hear!")

What This Means

I've rendered Saying 7 quite differently here, because most readers don't have lions on their everyday radar. The wording in most translations gets really confusing: If you eat a lion, it becomes human, but if a lion eats a human, it becomes human? Hold up. So regardless of which one eats the other, a lion turns human?

Plato and Philo would've gotten it and people in antiquity would probably have reached this connection with the lion, too. What it really concerns is *ferocity* and sheer *freedom*, which the king of the jungle possessed fully. *That* is a very good thing.

Nature has a built-in understanding of the Divine. It's completely wild and untamed, yet there's also a noticeable order to it. Humankind is part of nature, too, but not so much when *we* start playing God.

Here we find the first parable of the text, about the one who fishes, no less. It's something Jesus and his students were quite familiar with, since they lived and worked closely to the coast. Fishing was a way of life, although at the time it was getting tougher as trade was booming on the Sea of Galilee, making it more and more difficult to make a living.

The Teacher tells the story to exemplify a girl or woman (the gender doesn't matter) who was skilled at fishing. Most likely, it was her way of life, or at least her daily activity. It was right there, while doing what she always did, that she stumbled upon something from the deep. It was something more valuable than anything else, which led her to abandon the norm.

In Chinese philosophy, the concept of *xin* (心) combines both the heart and mind, literally "heartmind." It's the idea that understanding, intention, and one's feeling about something are all from one space. Emotions without intellect or using reason without reading the mood is a sign of an undeveloped or fragmented cognition. So, in the story here, this girl's got mad skills!

A helpful takeaway from the text would be how the small fish were like little, trivial matters, while perhaps what's actually caught is that big, extraordinary realization that *they* are One with Consciousness. That would be quite the catch! The girl "with all her heartmind" discovers what is of Real Value and lets go of the many little things which don't have any.

For the seeker, too, one may be doing what they always do when they simply stumble upon an Experience of Transformation which they, too, *know* that will shift things in a big, big way.

A note about parables, since there will be several of them: These allegorical pieces read in the Bible or Christian texts are probably closer to summaries or snippets hitting the main point of the teaching being given at the time rather than the entire story.

These parables and teachings may have gone on for hours, in provocative or subversive ways. They might have even gone back and forth in discussions between the speaker and the crowds. And it's highly improbable that one would have written down all the details and nuances between them — or that they were said exactly verbatim each time.

With that in mind, allow yourself to let the parables move you into deeper reflection, rather than assume they were shared as short snippets and then just moved right along to the next point.

Contemplative Reflection

How can we cultivate the "ferocity" and "freedom" of a lion in our own spiritual pursuits?

This question encourages us to reflect on how we can approach our spiritual journey with a greater sense of passion, determination, and courage. It challenges us to examine any limiting beliefs or fears that may be holding us back from fully embracing our spiritual potential apart from ego.

In what ways do we "play God" in our relationship with nature, and how can we cultivate a more harmonious and balanced approach?

This question prompts us to consider our role within the natural world and to examine how our actions may impact the delicate balance of the ecosystem. It encourages us to explore ways in which we can live in greater alignment with the natural order and to recognize the interconnectedness of all things.

FREEBIE:

We can cultivate the "heartmind" (our deeper understanding, intentions, and feelings) to determine what's really important in our lives.

Consider for a moment how *the Teacher* is using this first parable to show:

- The importance of aligning our thoughts, feelings, and intentions in our spiritual journey.
- The need to discern between what is truly valuable and what is merely trivial in our lives.
- The transformative power of realizing our Oneness with Consciousness.
- The possibility (or even probability) of stumbling upon this realization while engaged in our everyday activities. (Still, our net must be in the water. Right?)

This foundational understanding of Real Value and Oneness will be built upon throughout several upcoming teachings and parables.

Chapter 4 (Saying 9)
The Seeds of Awareness

9

"Consciousness is also like a worker who is walking along and planting seeds. He reaches into a bag and grabs a handful of seeds, which he flings.

"Some seeds land on the dirt path, where birds grab up and eat them all.

"Others hit solid rock. These might sprout a bit, but none are truly able to take root or mature.

"Some of the seeds, also, land under an invasive shrub which blocks the sunlight and chokes them out. These seeds become nothing more than food for the worms.

"But then again, there are some seeds that land on good soil and grow high up to the sky, producing plenty of fruit. Some even truckloads!"

(Standard Translation: Saying 9
Jesus said, "Look, a sower went out, took a handful of seeds, and scattered them. Some fell on the roadside; the birds came and gathered them. Others fell on the rock; they didn't take root in the soil and ears of grain didn't rise toward heaven. Yet others fell on thorns; they choked the seeds and worms ate them. Finally, others fell on good soil; it produced fruit up toward heaven, some sixty times as much and some a hundred and twenty.")

What This Means

The second parable of the "seed-flinger" also has a parallel version in the canonical gospels, just like the one with the person who was fishing.

Here's a worker who plants seeds, and seeds are being tossed indiscriminately.

One can argue that an actual farmer wouldn't be so careless, but instead would till the land, using proper spacing between seeds, the right amount of water, of nutrients... but *this ain't that guy.* This person is about doing what he does, just like the previous parable, and *he's sharing what he's got with the whole wide world.*

The students must have thought he was nuts, and perhaps he was. It wouldn't matter. After all, the Ultimate Reality (that is God) is not something to be understood superficially.

Some seeds landed on the roadside—a path both constructed by and trampled over by humans. Interesting how those didn't take, huh. Some seeds landed on the rocks—a densely rigid material where seeds could not possibly root deeply or grow strong.

Then, some seeds fell among the "thorns" as most translate it. The word in Coptic is ϣⲟⲛⲧⲉ. I guess it could mean thorn, but its Coptic usage is also found in reference to the *Acacias-nilotica*. This is a low-growing, desert shrub that would rob the ground of most of its nutrients that the seeds need while also blocking Light that would otherwise reach them. One really wouldn't want a seed to land in a dying and life-sucking community, where the most activity going on is by the worms, feeding off the corpses? These worms aren't the kinds of squiggly things that turn into beautiful butterflies. No. They're the kind that keel over themselves after a life of eating and pooping, and all of it becomes "food" for the greedy bush.

Finally, one sees that all is not wasted. Some of the seeds that this carefree soul is generously sharing *do* hit the right spot—where they bloom and grow in abundance, bearing fruit by the bushels.

Did you catch that? It's "sixty to a hundred and twenty-fold," or "truckload" as I word it. The point here is just as much about setting our intention without expectation and not doing stuff just with the "fruit" in mind. If you can let that go, the outcome is said to exceed our capacity to contain it.

"Be this seed-happy guy" is most likely the main point, but one can also benefit by considering the seed's perspective. What kind of substrate would you like to find yourselves in? What kind of heart must you have in order to receive and make use of it?

Food for thought...

Contemplative Reflection

What does the sower represent in this parable? How can we embody the sower's indiscriminate generosity and unwavering faith in the potential for growth?

This question encourages us to consider the sower as a metaphor for recognizing how Awareness "lands" on different types of people, as well our own approach to sharing spiritual teachings or engaging in acts of kindness towards others (and ourselves!). It prompts us to also reflect on the importance of releasing expectations and trusting in the inherent potential for positive change.

What could be these seeds that we are planting in our own lives and in the world around us? What kind of soil are we cultivating for these seeds to take root and flourish?

This question invites us to contemplate the nature of our actions, intentions, and the impact they have on our own growth and the well-being of others. It encourages us to examine the conditions we are creating for positive change and to consider how we can cultivate a more fertile environment for spiritual growth and flourishing in our own soul—er, I mean "soil."

Chapter 5 (Sayings 10 & 11)
Igniting Recognition

10

"I'm here to set fire to the entire world," the Teacher said, "Take a look and see how I'm very protective and attentive, caring for it until the flame starts to ignite and blaze up."

11

"If your eyes are fixed on the skies, you're being distracted. Don't be so preoccupied with heaven. It's simply the wrong place to look. Once we've become truly aware, there's no going back to that way of seeing things.

"It's not the dead who are Living, nor do the Living die. Devour what's dead and it's made alive—it's transmuted after being metabolized. Whenever one moves into the Light of Awareness, is this not what becomes of ego, what happens to our past perceptions?

"In Reality, we are One, but for some reason, we've fabricated this ideal of being separate, of being an *other*. If we do this, who do we think we are then, and where do we stop dividing things?"

> (Standard Translation: Saying 10
> Jesus said, "I've cast fire on the world, and look, I'm watching over it until it blazes."
>
> Saying 11
> Jesus said, "This heaven will disappear, and the one above it will disappear too. Those who are dead aren't alive, and those who are living won't die. In the days when you ate what was dead, you made it alive. When you're in the light, what will you do? On the day when you were one, you became divided. But when you become divided, what will you do?")

What This Means

The Teacher adds another concept, Fire. It's pre-elemental, the way it's described. Yet for *the Teacher*, this quality of Fire is not one of destruction—Jesus pushed for non-violent resistance that was very different from the brutal force his society operated in at the time. It's an aspect of Divine Energy which sparks Life itself. It also becomes a tool for continual spiritual illumination when properly attended.

In the next part, the text again shows how easy it is in religious circles to get caught up in the notion of "heaven is our home." There is an appeal of one day walking down streets of gold, to a mansion filled with crowns one has earned for all of eternity, with the sound of harp music in a continuous loop. But frankly, this view creates castes and hierarchy, superiors and inferiors, and more divisions.

There's no doubt that suffering here in the world has been around for a very long time, but the encouragement from *the Teacher* is that it's also intertwined with hope and peace that can be obtained right here and now. Once one has become "Aware of Awareness," perceiving the Unity of Oneness, there's just no unseeing it. Fire, too, ties back into that ferocity and freedom and balance we see in nature, like the lion. It indwells everything around us and is also imbued with the Divine. We are One with the Universe.

So why do we keep separating ourselves out of it? Why do we keep splitting *this* from *that* when by Divine design, it's all Connected?

Contemplative Reflection

What does *the Teacher* mean by "setting fire to the entire world"? How does this relate to the concept of spiritual illumination and transformation?

This question encourages deeper reflection on the metaphor of fire as a catalyst for change and renewal. It prompts us to consider how spiritual practices and insights can ignite a process of inner transformation that ultimately leads to a more awakened and interconnected way of being (or Be-ing).

How can we shift our focus from a preoccupation with heaven or "religious activity" to a deeper awareness of the present moment and the interconnectedness of all things?

This question challenges us to examine our own spiritual beliefs and practices. (Of course, this doesn't mean to just hastily chunk everything.) It invites us to consider how we can cultivate a more grounded and embodied spirituality that is rooted in the present moment and the recognition of the Divine within ourselves and the world around us.

Chapter 6 (Sayings 12 - 17)
Beyond Religion

12

The students asked another question. "Once you're gone, who's going to teach us?"

The Teacher said, "I'm afraid that you might still cling to whatever religious tradition you came from. They have promised you heaven apart from earth, and it all sounds nice and organized, right?"

13

"So," asked the Teacher, "Who would you compare me to?"

The student they called the Boulder said, "Definitely, an Angel sent from God!"

Another named the Unifying One said, "I'd say you are like a wise philosopher—or ancient sage!"

Yet the Twin said, "There's just no words to really explain it, Teacher."

"Look who's the teacher, now," the Teacher replied. "There is a Spring that gushes out from the Source, boiling over from the Fire. You seem to be getting drunk on what I've been serving."

The Teacher pulled the Twin aside and whispered three words. (*I AM Om.*)"

Afterwards, the others came up to the Twin. "What did the Teacher tell you?"

"I really can't tell you. Even if I did try to repeat any of it, you'd just hurl things at me in anger. But I'm telling you, that Fire would burst from the things and burn (within) you."

14

The Teacher said, "You do understand, don't you, that it's not about religious rules of any kind. There's nothing to prove by fasting or praying out loud or showing how generous to charities you are. All of this knocks you right off track. People will even scoff at you and judge you for doing it. What happens then is that you just end up bringing harm to yourself.

"Instead, consider what's going on as you go inwardly into the heartmind. See what you come across there. And just like you would do towards someone being hospitable to you, be gracious if it lets you inside, and accept what it has to offer. Heal those parts that need healing.

"You see, it's not what you can talk about that matters, but how you show yourself to be—and towards yourself as well—with humility, gratitude and compassion."

15

"Once you take a good, hard look at someone or some *thing* and can see the One, adore it."

16

"Some people might think that I'm just throwing around ideas about peace, but that's not what it's really about. I'm here to teach you how to think and live in a way which separates these ideologies from Reality, to take us from duality into Nonduality.

"Everything we've grown up being told—what to think, how to act, who you are, as well as what your own thoughts, feelings and ideas should be—must be deprogrammed. This way you can find your True Self once again, a kind of remembering in/as the One."

17

"I'm offering you this: There is One, who is beyond what you can see or hear or touch, beyond the conceivable or imagined."

(Standard Translation: Saying 12
The disciples said to Jesus, "We know you're going to leave us. Who will lead us then?"
Jesus said to them, "Wherever you are, you'll go to James the Just, for whom heaven and earth came into being."

Saying 13
Jesus said to his disciples, "If you were to compare me to someone, who would you say I'm like?"
Simon Peter said to him, "You're like a just angel."
Matthew said to him, "You're like a wise philosopher."
Thomas said to him, "Teacher, I'm completely unable to say whom you're like."
Jesus said, "I'm not your Teacher. Because you've drunk, you've become intoxicated by the bubbling spring I've measured out."
He took him aside and told him three things. When Thomas returned to his companions, they asked, "What did Jesus say to you?"
Thomas said to them, "If I tell you one of the things he said to me, you'll pick up stones

and cast them at me, and fire will come out of the stones and burn you up."

Saying 14

Jesus said to them, "If you fast, you'll bring guilt upon yourselves; and if you pray, you'll be condemned; and if you make donations, you'll harm your spirits.

"If they welcome you when you enter any land and go around in the countryside, heal those who are sick among them and eat whatever they give you, because it's not what goes into your mouth that will defile you. What comes out of your mouth is what will defile you."

Saying 15

Jesus said, "When you see the one who wasn't born of a woman, fall down on your face and worship that person. That's your Father."

Saying 16

Jesus said, "Maybe people think that I've come to cast peace on the world, and they don't know that I've come to cast divisions on the earth: fire, sword, and war. Where there are five in a house, there'll be three against two and two against three, father against and son and son against father. They'll stand up and be one."

Saying 17
Jesus said, "I'll give you what no eye has ever seen, no ear has ever heard, no hand has ever touched, and no human mind has ever thought.")

What This Means

There's a lot happening in this section, but it, too, is all connected. Promise.

It begins with the students asking another silly question. (There's so many of them!) At what point would Jesus have to think he might have solicited the wrong fellas? Maybe what *the Teacher*/Jesus thought was *if these guys get it, anyone can!* At any rate, they ask, and *the*

Teacher responds with another *I can't believe you're asking me this.*

It's worth noting here that most translators of the Gospel of Thomas seem to have given the disciples a free pass where Jesus told them that James the Just, his brother, would lead them. But then he added a rather weird "For whom all heaven and earth came into being." Huh? The original text reads ιακωβοc π ∆ικαιοc. This translates to "Jacob, who's righteous." The common usage of the word righteous in this ancient time was "observing of social rule, well ordered, and civilized." That's from Homer. Was Jesus taking a jab at James, who was known for insisting that Gentiles be fully converted to various Jewish rituals, too, such as circumcision? It kind of sounds like it.

This is the reason I think *the Teacher* (Jesus) could be giving them a bit of a poke here (like he often does throughout all of the gospels). He could be pointing to the "righteous" ways they were accustomed to, back in their old tradition, and then follows up with his own question: *Who exactly do you think I am?*

"An angel from God!" That is, you only look human, but really, you are absolutely divine. The meaning of the name Simon, the first student to speak up, is Listening or Hearing. Is Jesus using one of those ironic names "Like 'Tiny' over in vice," when nicknaming him Peter? That name means "rock" or "stone," which in early orthodoxy ties it to where Jesus is attributed with saying, "Upon this rock will I build my church." Although I think it can be argued that it's the kind of nickname that could just as likely reference something else, such as a stone that gets wielded like a weapon to be thrown at the accused, a rock that sinks when it tries to walk on water itself, maybe even like a primitive and blunt tool, or an obstacle easily piled up to make walls. Perhaps it just means someone who seems rather dense. Several instances throughout the gospels seem to agree. (I call him the Boulder here, and he will pop up even more in the section from the Gospel of Mary.)

The next student to answer the question (who they believe the *Teacher* to be) says, "The wisest of philosophers!" Like, you're so smart, probably the next Socrates or Plato. Levi's name means "To join in harmony" or "To make a connection." By his other name, Matthew, he's called "A gift from God." The gospel attributed to him also seems to try to bridge early conflicts between Jewish and Christian communities. His response seems to follow Peter's "You're from Heaven!" with "But also a great Human!" still trying to unite things. (He, too, has a brief appearance in the Gospel of Mary, where I also call him, the Unifying One.)

But then Thomas—remember, this is the *Twin*—comes back with, "There's no way to describe you," you're beyond it all. Seems the

Twin is of–like–mind and of–like–heart to *the Teacher.*

The manuscript doesn't really tell us the three words Jesus spoke. Whatever it was, it was enough that the others would cry out, *Blasphemy!*

One could claim—considering the Fire that comes from the Source—that it was perhaps something like "I am God," or "Thou art That," only in other words. If we look carefully at everything about Kingdom, Consciousness, Oneness, Reality as he's been teaching, it makes sense. A choice was made to combine the *I AM* (the Hebrew/Christian notion) with *Om* (the Hindu notion) not just because it's three words which I thought might be clever, but to convey that it *must* be something beyond one's particular religion's construct.

The Teacher continues this line of thought by telling the students that dogma and religious rituals bring about a degree of harm, and that true religion is more a matter of putting oneself out there in a way that brings healing and shows compassion to others. It has to do with getting completely caught up in Spirit, which follows what's countercurrent to mere religion.

The section continues by saying that we need to pay attention to and recognize Source in others. Find Unity in this. Then we need to look at how it's our ideologies that have caused division.

Even though these teachings of Oneness and of Ultimate Reality are something many will not want to hear, that is the offer. It's an invitation to go beyond our imagination, to share in the Divine.

It's said that during Buddha's last days, his disciples too asked who his successor would be.

Aatma Deepo Bhava. (आत्म: दीपो भव:) "Be a light unto yourself." Seems like *the Teacher* agrees.

Contemplative Reflection

What does *the Teacher's* response to the question about his successor reveal about his views on religious tradition and authority?

This question prompts us to consider why the Teacher expresses concern that his students might cling to their old religious traditions. It invites us to reflect on the potential limitations of relying solely on external authorities and the importance of cultivating a direct, personal experience of the Divine. (It can be tough letting go. I get it.)

How do the different responses of the students (*the Boulder, the Unifying One, the Twin*) reflect their varying levels of spiritual understanding, when asked, "Who would you compare me to?"

This question encourages us to examine how their answers reveal their unique understanding (or misunderstanding) of the Teacher's teachings. It prompts us to consider the depth our own interpretations of spiritual figures and teachings.

Chapter 7 (Sayings 18 & 19)
Beyond Conceptual Time

18

The students asked, "So, what's it like at the end—you know, like when we die?"

"Have you really figured out the beginning already," asked the Teacher, "since you're asking about the end? Because it's actually at the end where one must start from, right?

"A shout out to the one who takes a good, hard look at the *very* beginning. They're the ones who will find stability in transcendence, right there at the end, and true death will be undone."

19

"That's right, way to go! They are the ones who are filled with Awareness, even before they become aware of it.

"Anyone who learns from me—really paying attention to what I'm saying—will soon discover they can learn as well from anything.

"This way is different from trying to examine or understand spirituality with man–made and dualistic concepts. That way is dead. True Reality has no beginning and no end. It is only to be *known*."

(Standard Translation: Saying 18
The disciples said to Jesus, "Tell us about our end. How will it come?"

Jesus said, "Have you discovered the beginning so that you can look for the end? Because the end will be where the beginning is. Blessed is the one who will stand up in the beginning. They'll know the end, and won't taste death."

Saying 19
Jesus said, "Blessed is the one who came into being before coming into being. If you become my disciples and listen to my message, these stones will become your

servants; because there are five trees in paradise which don't change in summer or winter, and their leaves don't fall. Whoever knows them won't taste death.")

What This Means

The Teacher must be going through everything in his head, trying to figure out why the students are not understanding what "the end of the journey" is. *Maybe they're still stuck on the metaphor about old people and infants? Dang. Betcha I'm gonna hafta repeat all this other stuff, aren't I...* (Yup. You sure are.)

If only *the Teacher* had been born several centuries later. He could then have just quoted T. S. Eliot's bit from *Four Quartets, No. 4.V*:

> "With the drawing of this Love and the
> voice of this Calling
> We shall not cease from exploration
> And the end of all our exploring

68

Will be to arrive where we started

And know the place for the first time."

Alas, he does well enough on his own, as *the Teacher* starts with coming into that big, capital "A" Awareness where one reaches a point of Enlightenment. It's that moment of experiencing God in–and–as everything, including what you can't see. It is there. God will teach you.

One might wonder: Does this include religion or philosophy, which between the various beliefs, denominations, and schools of thought, all seem to differ greatly? To be honest, it does, but that's not to say that God is behind every individual concept, every single thought. Nor does it mean that "every word in the Bible" is independently something we can learn from when it's separated from its cultural context, its audience, author, and literary genre. That leads to serious trouble.

It's been rightly said, "The finger pointing to the moon (or reflection in the pond of the moon) is not the moon," and "The map is not the path." *The Teacher* cautions against blindly believing in what a person thinks or what they claim to be Truth, throughout several Sayings.

The last half of logion 19 is tricky and has been reworked here for clarity. Standard translations are quite different and somewhat confusing, similar to how "The lion eats man and becomes man" earlier.

Stones will serve you? Five trees in Paradise? Only two seasons?

Here is where some context helps. Any which way you try to explain the word–for–word Coptic or Greek, one winds up holding stones that (translated literally word for word is) "will make–be serve to–you." Is it really so unusual for *the Teacher* to be saying something sarcastic (again)? Could it not refer to how God imbues even some stones and can teach directly with anything? *The Teacher* also shows us elsewhere how we're not dependent on people who are in higher spiritual positions or solely through the God-inspired scriptures or Christian books. Even though they may be helpful, they are also at times manipulated and used harmfully. It's why *the Teacher* speaks about discernment all throughout the manuscript.

What about trees in Paradise? Whether they are five, or something like a Tree of Life or a Tree of Knowledge of Good and Evil (who knows?), what's clear is that they are all about religious myth. Another aspect of this saying is how it speaks to the fact that these trees don't change. "Oh, so they're evergreens? Paradise has pines?" I don't think that's the point.

When one looks at winter and summer—which leaves out the third season that Egypt has, spring, each being four months long—one should notice that these seasons mentioned are those where trees are fruitless, or dead.

If we say that one is *in the know* of this state of Paradise, it places *you* smack dab in the right season: the one where we find growth and bear fruit.

Contemplative Reflection

What does *the Teacher* mean when he says, "It's actually at the end where one must start from"? How does this perspective challenge our usual understanding of beginnings and endings?

This question invites us to consider the cyclical nature of existence and the possibility that the "end" of our journey may, in fact, be a return to our original state of being. It encourages us to explore deeper concepts like the "death" of ignorance, ego, or paradigm, as a transition and a potential for renewal. (Tread softly, since some of these guys don't go down so easily.)

How can we cultivate the kind of awareness that allows us to "learn from anything"? What does it mean to approach the world with a beginner's mind and an openness to the inherent wisdom of all things?

The prompt here is a challenge for us to expand our understanding of what constitutes a "teacher" and to recognize the potential for learning and growth in every experience. It urges us to consider how we can cultivate a sense of curiosity and openness that allows us to receive the teachings that are present in every moment.

Chapter 8 (Sayings 20 & 21)
Cultivation and Keenness

20

The students asked, "Can you explain to us what this True Reality is like?"

"It would be similar to the smallest kind of seed there is," the Teacher said, "and how when it has landed on well cultivated soil, it grows and becomes a large, strong plant. One so strong that the birds of the sky would perch and even nest there, and they would be protected from predators, and from those that claim the tree is theirs alone."

21

A woman the Teacher called the Tower asked, "Ideally, what would any of your students be like?"

The Teacher smiled, "To most people, they would seem like little kids playing in a field on someone else's property. When the owner comes up to them, they reveal their True Selves saying, 'Leave this spot, it is ours.' And the owner does.

"You must try to understand what it means to become completely aware. After all, there are those who will try to steal what you have, so stay strong and ready. It will be necessary for you to grow in knowledge and to apply it quickly, just as you would with a delicious piece of fruit. Pick it and eat it while it's ripe. Otherwise, it's not any good."

(Standard Translation: Saying 20
The disciples asked Jesus, "Tell us, what can the kingdom of heaven be compared to?"
He said to them, "It can be compared to a mustard seed. Though it's the smallest of all the seeds, when it falls on tilled soil it makes a plant so large that it shelters the birds of heaven."

Saying 21

Mary said to Jesus, "Whom are your disciples like?"

He said, "They're like little children living in a field which isn't theirs. When the owners of the field come, they'll say, 'Give our field back to us.' They'll strip naked in front of them to let them have it and give them their field.

"So I say that if the owner of the house realizes the bandit is coming, they'll watch out beforehand and won't let the bandit break into the house of their domain and steal their possessions. You, then, watch out for the world! Prepare to defend yourself so that the bandits don't attack you, because what you're expecting will come. May there be a wise person among you!

"When the fruit ripened, the reaper came quickly, sickle in hand, and harvested it. Anyone who has ears to hear should hear!")

What This Means

Are the students starting to catch on? *Okay. We admit it. We've been jumping the gun. So how 'bout this one: Can you explain Ultimate Reality again? It's on our inside and our outside or... what was it again?*

The Teacher explains, but only the part they would likely get—at least for the time being.

He explains the growing movement of the tree's trunk and branches which continually penetrate the plane and spread out. It has the ability to sustain and protect—and even nourish—life here in the material world. (That's stunningly beautiful, right?) The Kingdom which Jesus speaks of is like this, too. It's not way *up there in heaven* or somewhere *out there*, nor is it *down here on Earth*, concerned with conquering, ruling, demanding allegiance, or enslaving us (politically or religiously). I would bet that they were not expecting to hear this.

The text is honestly unclear about the next person asking a question. It's attributed to a *Mariham/Mary.* If so, which Mary would that be? The Bible mentions a myriad of Marys. Anna Cwikla (a scholar and expert in the field of Marys), states that probably one in every four women during the time of Jesus may have shared the name.

The Coptic word in the original text is ⲘⲀⲣⲓⲋⲀⲘ and could have just as easily been translated "craftsman," or better: ''One who bears witness." (Whoa; I really like that!) What we do know is that it's the same name and spelling as the woman considered as Mary Magdalene in Saying 114, of which Magdala means the "high tower."

What is clear however is that the person wondered what kind of student *the Teacher* had hoped to have. (Surely this would have cracked *the Teacher* up, don't you think?)

At first glance, it seems Jesus answers that his ideal students are these young, trespassing hoodlums that bully the property owner away. How is this possibly one's *ideal* student?

If one ponders this for a moment, we can reasonably assume that *the Teacher* understands the value of a child-like innocence. After all, it's a lack of inhibition and sincerity of faith that is needed to approach Reality without preconception or indoctrination. Right?

It's also worth considering that by all of society's rights, the land belonged to the person who purchased it, even from a line of previous owners and so on, until we reach the person who first sets claim to it. And that's where I think it gets interesting. In Reality, however, the land is actually *owned by no one—* and it's cared for by all.

What's even more intriguing is that *the Teacher* continues by asking for our attention in this next part, warning us that there will be those who are dead set on staking their claim on something. It could be land, or it could even be concepts such as God or salvation, on who belongs and who doesn't, or on what rules must be followed. *This* is what *the Teacher* warns us about. *Be ready for this.*

One must be sure of the Truth that one Knows, devouring it and digesting it as soon as it's made available. Ignore this and there's "hell" to pay.

Contemplative Reflection

How does the parable of the mustard seed relate to the concept of True Reality? What does it teach us about the potential for spiritual growth and the expansive nature of Consciousness?

This question encourages us to explore the symbolism of the mustard seed as a representation of True Reality. It prompts us to consider how even the smallest seed of spiritual awareness can, when nurtured and cultivated, grow into a powerful and expansive force for good. (And perhaps even how the misperception that's labelled as "size" truly doesn't matter!)

What does *the Teacher's* vision of the ideal student reveal about the nature of spiritual awareness and the challenges of embodying one's True Self in the world?

This question invites us to reflect on some of the qualities of an ideal student as described by the Teacher. It challenges us to consider how we can cultivate a childlike "pre-programming" and inhibition. We can build a newer and stronger sense of self-awareness, and a willingness to challenge societal norms and expectations in order to live in alignment with our True Self. (And by all means, dump those "labels"!)

Chapter 9 (Sayings 22 & 23)
Beyond the Senses

22

The Teacher noticed a mother breastfeeding her child and turned to the students, "A nursing baby is like those who go inward in order to perceive Consciousness."

"What do you mean? How does someone turn into a child again? Maybe think like a little kid?" they asked.

"When you are able to let go of your separateness and integrate yourself as the One," said the Teacher, "and you understand that inside and outside are One, Spirit and matter One, man and woman, male and female, One. It is like that.

"From what (Who) are you able to listen? Change how you see, how you touch and move, change the form, and then you will be able to perceive Consciousness."

23

"There's no special treatment for some, but punishment for others. There is only realizing that it's all One."

(Standard Translation: Saying 22
Jesus saw some little children nursing. He said to his disciples, "These nursing children can be compared to those who enter the kingdom."
They said to him, "Then we'll enter the kingdom as little children?"
Jesus said to them, "When you make the two into one, and make the inner like the outer and the outer like the inner, and the upper like the lower, and so make the male and the female a single one so that the male won't be male nor the female female; when you make eyes in the place of an eye, a hand in the place of a hand, a foot in the place of a foot, and an image in the place of an image; then you'll enter the kingdom."

Saying 23

Jesus said, "I'll choose you, one out of a thousand and two out of ten thousand, and they'll stand as a single one.")

What This Means

This section has a rare setup of a "story." It goes something like this: *The Teacher* sees both a nursing mother and an opportunity to give an object lesson. *Maybe the fellas just aren't so good at learning by listening. Hey, here's something I can teach them visually. "A nursing infant is like one who gets what God/Consciousness is..."*

(How frustrating would it be to you if your students took away from that, "Huh? We gotta turn back into babies?" I can hear the palm slapping of my forehead now. But *the Teacher* shows a bit of grace by explaining it again.)

The infant does not perceive their mother as separate, or the milk as separate. When it's missing mother or milk, it knows something's off. When one uses spiritual organs (different from sensory ones), they perceive All and recognize All is as it should be—inward and outward, male and female, you and me, All One.

How do we do this? The standard translation says, "when you make eyes in the place of an eye, a hand in the place of a hand, a foot in the place of a foot, and an image in the place of an image; then you'll enter the kingdom." It is similar to the start of the Kena Upanishad (part one, verse two) where it answers:

श्रोत्रस्य श्रोत्रं मनसो मनो यद्वाचो ह वाचं स उ प्राणस्य प्राणश्चक्षुषश्चक्षुः   ।
अतिमुच्य धीराः प्रेत्यास्माल्लोकादमृता भवन्ति ॥

śrotrasya śrotram manaso mano yadvāco ha vācaṃ sa u prāṇasya prāṇaścakṣuṣaścakṣuḥ |
atimucya dhīrāḥ pretyāsmāllokādamṛtā bhavanti ||

It is the ear of the ear, mind of the mind, tongue of the tongue, and life of the life and eye of the eye. Being disabused of the false notion, the wise, having left this body, become immortal.

That is, it's not the ear that hears. It's as Shankara explains, " '...what intelligent Being directs the mind and the other senses towards their respective objects, and how it directs them.' Ear is that by which one hears, *i.e.*, the sense whose function is to hear sounds and distinguish them. He, you asked for, is the ear of that."

The next Saying (23) is typically translated as: "I'll choose you, one out of a thousand and two out of ten thousand..." It sounds familiar, as from Deuteronomy 32:30, but it would be strange to place it here since the chapter in Deuteronomy is all about God's unhinged wrath. *The Teacher's* playing with us again. It makes no sense to say one or two are picked while thousands are not. That's not Unity at all.

It should be noted that in the original Coptic text, there is a *lacunae* or hole on this part where "choose" is. Maybe something important is missing, maybe not.

What is interesting is that the very next statement that also aligns with Jesus' typical anti-specialness view: "Standing on their feet singularly as One." No distinction. No separation. And the entire text is rather replete with similar anti-specialness language as one sees it.

But, if *one out of a thousand and two out of ten thousand* is not sarcasm, then something important is missing right before the lacunae. Personally, I'll put my money on *the Teacher's* wit and sarcasm every time. The meaning would not contradict everything else he's taught. *You guys are one in a million! (Wink!)*

Contemplative Reflection

How can we cultivate a sense of "oneness" and interconnectedness, as exemplified by the nursing baby's relationship with its mother? What practices or perspectives might help us dissolve the illusion of separateness?

This question invites us to reflect on the nature of our relationships and how we can cultivate a deeper sense of connection and interdependence. It encourages us to explore practices that can help us shift our perspective from a sense of isolation to a recognition of our inherent unity with all things.

What does *the Teacher* mean by "change how you see, how you touch and move, change the form"? How can we transform our perception and experience of reality in order to perceive Consciousness more fully?

This question challenges us to consider the ways in which our habitual patterns of perception and behavior may limit our understanding of reality. It encourages us to explore practices that can help us expand our awareness, shift our perspective, and open ourselves to a more direct experience of Consciousness.

Chapter 10 (Sayings 24 - 29)
The Heart of Reality

24

The students said, "Please, explain to us where your teachings are coming from. It's really hard to figure it out!"

The Teacher said, "You must listen from the Heart. There is Light from within that shines on everything. Of course, when you aren't using this Light, it's only darkness."

25

"Show love to others, just as you would show love for your own Soul. Look after them, protecting and caring for them just as you would with your own eye."

26

"Why do you seem so bothered, nitpicking over the smallest thing about others? You've got bigger issues which are blocking your own clear view of them. Deal with those first, and then you can approach others."

27

"If you don't step back from what is merely physical, you'll never REALize REALity. If you ignore how everything is deeply connected, the Source will stay undiscovered."

28

"I am standing right here in plain sight, in the middle of everything, and it's like everyone is drunk and couldn't care less. No one is driven to go deeper. How heartbreaking it is to see how completely distracted people are. They're so disinterested in anything meaningful. If only they would wake up, they would find their Selves."

29

"Those who believe that everything physical actually just pops up from a non-corporeal Consciousness can feel amazed by it. And those who get stuck in their heads can feel shocked thinking about how their mind creates everything, including the very illusion one *thinks* is real.

"What perplexes me is how a human being, as magnificent and complex as one is, can get in such a rut spending all their time and attention wondering if we are spirits trapped in a body or bodies that contrive a spirit, instead of just living fully in both body and spirit."

(Standard Translation: Saying 24
His disciples said, "Show us the place where you are, because we need to look for it."
He said to them, "Anyone who has ears to hear should hear! Light exists within a person of light, and they light up the whole world. If they don't shine, there's darkness."

Saying 25
Jesus said, "Love your brother as your own soul. Protect them like the pupil of your eye."

Saying 26

Jesus said, "You see the speck that's in your brother's eye, but you don't see the beam in your own eye. When you get the beam out of your own eye, then you'll be able to see clearly to get the speck out of your brother's eye."

Saying 27

"If you don't fast from the world, you won't find the kingdom. If you don't make the Sabbath into a Sabbath, you won't see the Father."

Saying 28

Jesus said, "I stood in the middle of the world and appeared to them in the flesh. I found them all drunk; I didn't find any of them thirsty. My soul ached for the children of humanity, because they were blind in their hearts and couldn't see. They came into the world empty and plan on leaving the world empty. Meanwhile, they're drunk. When they shake off their wine, then they'll change."

Saying 29

Jesus said, "If the flesh came into existence because of spirit, that's amazing. If spirit came into existence because of the body, that's really amazing! But I'm amazed at how such great wealth has been placed in this poverty.")

What This Means

The Teacher instructs the students how they need the Light to see how to move into that next step of perceiving Ultimate Reality. They need to be able to discern where the facades are, too. In the original manuscript, it says "if you don't fast from the world, you won't find the Kingdom..." or as *the Teacher* would put it: *If you're so dead set on fasting, then fast the World, its ideologies, its doctrines, that kind of stuff.* From there, the original text goes on to say, "make the Sabbath into a Sabbath."

The phrase used here: ⲈⲒⲢⲈ ⲙ̄ ⲡ ⲤⲀⲘⲂⲀⲦⲞⲚ ⲛ̄ ⲤⲀⲃˋⲂⲀⲦⲞⲚ, is really "To make the Sabbath into a sABBAth." That is, *Father*-ize it! It's a clever play on words that is rendered here as: "REALize REALity." (I just couldn't help myself!)

The Teacher then connects this with what we see in the beginning of the text. We seek, become unsettled, then filled with wonder encountering God. It's a reminder that one is both magnificently human *and* Spirit, the Living Manifestation of the Living Source. *On earth as it is in heaven,* because the body *and* the world are wonderful. After all, this is the physical dwelling place of Spirit.

Later in the text, it even talks about how physicality has no independent value *above* anything else, but right here the point is that it begins with richness and poverty sharing the same space. It's all about harmony, which will be echoed again and again, and throughout the

94

Gospel of Mary as well. But let's not get too much ahead of ourselves. It's a nice segue into this next part, where *the Teacher* admonishes those who try to set limits on anyone's experiences with the Divine...

Contemplative Reflection

How can we cultivate the practice of "listening from the Heart"? What does it mean to access the "Light from within" that illuminates all things?

This question encourages us to explore the concept of inner wisdom and intuition. It prompts us to consider how we can cultivate a deeper connection to our own inner knowing and use this "Light" to guide our understanding and actions.

In what ways are we "drunk" or "distracted" in our daily lives? How can we awaken to a deeper sense of meaning and purpose, as *the Teacher* suggests? Could this help our understanding of what it means to live integrated and "embodied?"

This question challenges us to examine our own habits and behaviors. It invites us to consider how we might be missing out on a deeper experience of life due to distractions, busyness, or a lack of awareness. It encourages us to explore practices that can help us "wake up" and discover our True Self.

Chapter 11 (Sayings 30 - 36)
Beyond Trials and the Trival

30

"Anywhere you come across spiritual 'gatekeepers,' it's only the little-god banter of pretenders on a power trip. But if you find your Self—your True Self—having realized your Oneness, it's there you will find me, too."

31

"Often it's difficult for others who think they know you to understand the real you. It's like going to a therapist who happens to be an old family friend. They struggle to make any assessments without presumptions and projections."

32

"The one who is on top of the hill has an advantage of viewpoint and ability to defend.

However, they're also more exposed and easier to target."

33

"It's the same thing with whatever you have come to understand deep in your heart. You shouldn't feel like you have to hide it. Let it shine through you! It would be useless if you hooked up a porch light, only to then cover over it and never turn it on. No! You put it right on the Path, so that others can see it plainly and move along safely."

34

"In the same way, we don't expect a complete beginner with no experience to be the expedition guide for another newbie. When the Light is still too diffused, they'll both just get lost, stumble and fall, perhaps right off a cliff or into danger!"

35

"Sometimes we find ourselves facing a bad habit that just keeps getting in the way of going deeper. The obstacle is like a big thug, and there's no way to get inside the house to deal with it. So, what can be done?

"One must first use whatever strength they have to draw the thug outside in the open and all exposed. Restrained there, one can enter unharmed, turning the house inside out."

36

"It's important to realize that you cannot deal with anything when you're preoccupied with trivial things such as meals, clothing, and busywork. These shouldn't be so distracting."

(Standard Translation: Saying 30
Jesus said, "Where there are three deities, they're divine. Where there are two or one, I'm with them."

Saying 31

Jesus said, "No prophet is welcome in their own village. No doctor heals those who know them."

Saying 32

Jesus said, "A city built and fortified on a high mountain can't fall, nor can it be hidden."

Saying 33

Jesus said, "What you hear with one ear, listen to with both, then proclaim from your rooftops. No one lights a lamp and puts it under a basket or in a hidden place. Rather, they put it on the stand so that everyone who comes and goes can see its light."

Saying 34

Jesus said, "If someone who's blind leads someone else who's blind, both of them fall into a pit."

Saying 35

Jesus said, "No one can break into the house of the strong and take it by force without tying the hands of the strong. Then they can loot the house."

Saying 36
Jesus said, "Don't be anxious from morning to evening or from evening to morning about what you'll wear.")

What This Means

Here, I think the standard translation is a bit confusing: where there's three gods, or two or one... But we're not talking about the Trinity here. There's no *Theos* referenced. The Coptic reads ⲘⲀ ⲈⲨⲚ ⲰⲞⲘⲦ Ⲛ ⲚⲞⲨⲦⲈ , that is, "At the place (just your average *place*, really; nothing special) there are three (or any number of so-called) gods..." and goes on to say, "Well, that's where the gods are; they're just there (to paraphrase it). But where there's two or one (no mention of gods, and inferring a singular person), that is where I myself exist." *We are the Oneness, my friend.*

It's also clear that *the Teacher* knows there are dangers lurking in cultural society, but it can be this way with religious society, too. There are all these people out there telling you what's best for you, but it's just an act. For that matter, they may also be tricking themselves. Meanwhile, even *the Teacher* makes no claim to having any kind of superior role. You see, *you* can go direct to God yourself. You can discover your True Self yourself. And there's the answer to *"Where does all this come from, bruh? I told you, and I'm right there, too!"*

But that's not to say that it's going to be easy. Society, friends, family, all think they know who we are. They've seen us our whole lives, at least on the surface level. But there's more to us, right? As Jean-Yves Leloup, a wonderful theologian and translator, says of the *pure of heart* from the Beatitudes, "To see the Other, our vision must be emptied of presumptions and judgements."

Here, the text brings us back to that Light within. For those who have eyes to see, it shines brightly. For others, who are blind to it, there is the danger of stumbling or falling into more darkness. *I'm begging you, don't look to them for guidance.*

The Teacher also explains what to do when we come face to face with a bad habit, a vice, a character flaw. Some things just get in the way of spiritual growth and of healing ourselves. We struggle in meditating for more than three short minutes, reacting instead of mindfully responding. We grapple with motivation, with empathy. It doesn't have to be a full-blown addiction (although it could be that, too). The obstacle grows larger by the day, stronger by the minute, and suddenly one finds they are stuck. *The Teacher* drops a big hint here: *Don't try to overpower it on its own turf, that is, in your thoughts. Call it out for what it is.*

What one discovers out in the open is an imbalance, not a root evil. Do the heart work, even starting small or taking time to build up, and these spiritual practices can help move us out of being stuck in our heads. Let go of that separateness and integrate yourself as the One (as in Saying 22). It often takes giving grace to ourselves, too.

The text then tells one not to sweat the small stuff that's just on the surface. I mean, who needs that kind of distraction?

Contemplative Reflection

How can we discern between genuine spiritual teachers and "spiritual gatekeepers" who may be motivated by power or ego? What qualities should we look for in a true spiritual guide?

This question encourages us to critically examine those who present themselves as spiritual authorities. It prompts us to consider the importance of discernment and to seek out teachers who embody the qualities of humility, authenticity, and a genuine commitment to service.

How can we "let our light shine" and share our spiritual insights with others without fear of judgment or rejection? What does it mean to be a "lamp on the path" for those who are seeking guidance?

This question challenges us to overcome any hesitation or fear we may have about expressing our spiritual beliefs and experiences. It invites us to consider how we can share our light with the world in a way that is both authentic and compassionate.

What are some of the "bad habits" that may be hindering our spiritual growth? How can we use the Teacher's advice to "draw the thug outside" and confront these obstacles in order to create space for inner transformation?

This question encourages us to reflect on our own patterns of behavior and identify any areas where we may be getting stuck or holding ourselves back. It prompts us to consider how we can use mindfulness and self-awareness to address these challenges and create a more open and receptive inner environment.

Chapter 12 (Sayings 37 - 42)
Maturity and the Mainstream

37

The students asked, "When are you going to explain exactly who you really are?"

"When you stop pretending, and you rip off your own mask and throw it down, stomping it to pieces like a little kid would," replied the Teacher, "Only then will you be able to take a brave look at me. It may even shock you when you see only a child who belongs to the Oneness."

38

"You are constantly asking me to teach you, and I can't stand that you have no one else to learn from. You know I won't be with you forever."

39

"Yet here we are surrounded by all these spiritual leaders and religious scholars—they all have access to Ultimate Reality but won't go deeply themselves. What's worse, they do nothing to help others find it! So, you will have to become wise and gentle doing this yourselves."

40

"You see, a seedling that is planted close to the surface and is not tapped into the deeper Source will not grow strong. It's pulled up too easily and dies."

41

"You've heard how 'the rich get richer while the poor get poorer.' That is the way of societies."

42

"It's so important for one to be their True Self and not to get caught up in just following the crowd or trend."

(Standard Translation: Saying 37
His disciples said, "When will you appear to us? When will we see you?"
Jesus said, "When you strip naked without being ashamed, and throw your clothes on the ground and stomp on them as little children would, then you'll see the Son of the Living One and won't be afraid."

Saying 38
Jesus said, "Often you've wanted to hear this message that I'm telling you, and you don't have anyone else from whom to hear it. There will be days when you'll look for me, but you won't be able to find me."

Saying 39
Jesus said, "The Pharisees and the scholars have taken the keys of knowledge and hidden them. They haven't entered, and

haven't let others enter who wanted to. So be wise as serpents and innocent as doves."

Saying 40
Jesus said, "A grapevine has been planted outside of the Father. Since it's malnourished, it'll be pulled up by its root and destroyed."

Saying 41
Jesus said, "Whoever has something in hand will be given more, but whoever doesn't have anything will lose even what little they do have."

Saying 42
Jesus said, "Become passersby.")

What This Means

The students are still asking questions. This one, too, is it earnest? Are the students starting to go a little deeper, finally? It kind of seems they are realizing these teachings are vital.

The Teacher is deeply concerned that they're not hearing this from anywhere else. Of course, the message is constantly to look within, not to teachers or guides—but honestly, this is exactly the kind of guidance that they should be hearing from every spiritual leader.

It's obvious throughout all of the gospels—including this one—that Jesus knows his window of opportunity is small. As soon as he begins teaching these Truths, he becomes an immediate threat both to empire and religious groups. And he doesn't hold his punches with them, either. He blames the spiritual leaders that what he's teaching is totally unknown to people.

Once again, the students are told not to get distracted, but to focus on their own connection with the Divine since others offer no help.

Contemplative Reflection

What does *the Teacher* mean by "stop pretending" and "rip off your own mask"? How do these actions relate to the process of self-discovery and spiritual awakening?

This question encourages us to reflect on the ways in which we may be hiding our true selves behind social masks or personas. It invites us to consider how authenticity and vulnerability can lead to a deeper understanding of ourselves and our connection to the Divine.

Why does *the Teacher* express frustration that the students have "no one else to learn from"? What does this reveal about the importance of responsible, independent spiritual inquiry and the limitations of relying solely on external authorities?

This question challenges us to consider the importance of taking responsibility for our own spiritual growth and development. It prompts us to explore the potential pitfalls of blindly following religious or spiritual leaders and to cultivate our own inner wisdom and discernment.

How does the parable of the seedling relate to the concept of the "deeper Source"? What does it teach us about the importance of grounding our spiritual practice in a deep connection to the Divine?

This question encourages us to reflect on the metaphor of the seedling as a representation of our own spiritual journey. It invites us to consider how we can cultivate a strong and resilient spiritual practice by tapping into the "deeper Source" of wisdom and nourishment that lies within us and all of creation.

Chapter 13 (Sayings 43 - 45)
Intentions and Actions

43

"Can you remind us what kind of credentials you have to be saying all of this?" the students asked.

"Why would this even matter? Do you really not understand a single thing that I'm saying?" the Teacher replied.

"Don't be like those whiny, religious hypocrites, who love a tree, but hate its Fruit, or they love the fruit, but can't stand the kind of Tree that it comes from."

44

"One can be dismissive of any organization, its leaders or even what it teaches, and it won't matter all that much. Likewise, one might not fit in with its community or followers, and that's not such a big deal either. But if one disregards Source, then no real good can be done—not for oneself, not for others, not spiritually, and not even in their simple, everyday life."

45
"In the exact same way that one can't pick apples from a holly bush or grapes from sticker weeds, there's no way to harvest any good fruit from the wrong kind of habits and intentions. What you have is flavorless and without any nutrition.

"Only truly good people who have kindness, gentleness, compassion, patience and so on, already 'stored up' in their hearts, will bring about anything beneficial. Others who speak and behave in harmful ways do this because that's what has been stored up inside of them."

(Standard Translation: Saying 43
His disciples said to him, "Who are you to say these things to us?"

"You don't realize who I am from what I say to you, but you've become like those Judeans who either love the tree but hate its fruit, or love the fruit but hate the tree."

Saying 44
Jesus said, "Whoever blasphemes the Father will be forgiven, and whoever blasphemes the Son will be forgiven, but whoever blasphemes the Holy Spirit will not be forgiven, neither on earth nor in heaven."

Saying 45
Jesus said, "Grapes aren't harvested from thorns, nor are figs gathered from thistles, because they don't produce fruit. A person who's good brings good things out of their treasure, and a person who's evil brings evil things out of their evil treasure. They say evil things because their heart is full of evil.")

What This Means

Well, that answers the question about whether the students are starting to let go and get it yet or not. "Can we take a look at your resume, degrees, awards, anything?"

Facepalm. *Are you kidding me? Do you not see how hypocritical and haughty these guys are?*

I'm guessing *the Teacher* is pointing out how everyone (even his students) just love to be seen following something like a popular guru, but not to the point of making much effort to actually understand any of it. Or on the flip side, they claim to be spiritual, but hate that it's coming from this lay-person *Teacher*, not an ordained leader.

However, it's important to realize that consequences really matter. Does it help one's True Self by being in the right political party or a key member of the local megachurch? Not really. How about by being part of the "in crowd," the popular kids, or perhaps by being a highly valued volunteer? Nope.

But if one ignores or denies the Spirit, Source, Oneness, well that's different. They're not even capable of understanding anything that truly matters. Ouch.

The proof is right here in front of our faces. Everything is the by-product of the heart. If one taps into a fresh spring, out flows the refreshing water. Tap into sewage, into rotting waste, and what comes out is... well, nothing "refreshing."

Contemplative Reflection

What does *the Teacher* mean by the analogy of loving the tree but hating its fruit, or loving the fruit but hating the tree? How does this relate to the importance of our own integrity in our spiritual beliefs and practices?

This question invites us to reflect on the potential for hypocrisy in our spiritual lives. It challenges us to examine whether our actions and behaviors align with our professed beliefs and values.

How can we cultivate the "goodness" that *the Teacher* speaks of, characterized by kindness, gentleness, compassion, and patience? What practices or perspectives might help us embody these qualities more fully in our daily lives?

This question encourages us to consider the inner qualities that are essential for spiritual growth and flourishing. It prompts us to explore ways in which we can cultivate these virtues through practices such as mindfulness, self-reflection, and service to others.

Chapter 14 (Sayings 46 - 50)
The Way of Oneness

46

The Teacher said, "My own teacher was completely dedicated to Truth and Reality, and never shrank away from threats. Yet the person who has even just started to realize their True Self will see Reality at that same level that my teacher understood."

47

"You know, one cannot move forward along two different paths, navigating them both simultaneously. They can only give one path their honest attention. The same thing happens when one uses methods that were intended for past objectives in newer circumstances which have obviously changed. One can't just project modern meanings onto past perspectives, either. It's like an ill-fitting, patched-up jacket that will tear as soon as you move your arms."

48

"Of course, there might be times when different understandings coincide with each other, revealing the same Truth. It's great when this happens. There is both unity and strength in it that makes daunting things quite doable instead."

49

"Good things come to those who choose to recognize Oneness. They equally come from and return to Consciousness."

50

"Should anyone ask us where we come from, tell them this: 'We are from Pure Awareness, where the Light of Consciousness expresses itself, even as everything that we perceive.' And if they ask for proof, we can point to movement and stillness, itself."

(Standard Translation: Saying 46
Jesus said, "From Adam to John the Baptizer, no one's been born who's so much greater

than John the Baptizer that they shouldn't avert their eyes. But I say that whoever among you will become a little child will know the kingdom and become greater than John."

Saying 47

Jesus said, "It's not possible for anyone to mount two horses or stretch two bows, and it's not possible for a servant to follow two leaders, because they'll respect one and despise the other.

"No one drinks old wine and immediately wants to drink new wine. And new wine isn't put in old wineskins, because they'd burst. Nor is old wine put in new wineskins, because it'd spoil.

"A new patch of cloth isn't sewn onto an old coat, because it'd tear apart."

Saying 48

Jesus said, "If two make peace with each other in a single house, they'll say to the mountain, 'Go away,' and it will."

Saying 49

Jesus said, "Blessed are those who are one –
those who are chosen, because you'll find
the kingdom. You've come from there and
will return there."

Saying 50

Jesus said, "If they ask you, 'Where do you
come from?' tell them, 'We've come from
the light, the place where light came into
being by itself, established itself, and
appeared in their image.'

"If they ask you, 'Is it you?' then say, 'We are
its children, and we're chosen by our living
Father.'

"If they ask you, 'What's the sign of your
Father in you?' then say, 'It's movement and
rest.' ")

What This Means

Both the original and commonly translated text
references Jesus' admiration of John the
Baptist. By all accounts, he was someone who
influenced Jesus, having several qualities he

admired. What we really see here is that Jesus reinforces equality above hierarchy.

The Teacher continues by warning his students not to be swayed by societal, political, or spiritual "gangs." *See how they're all heading in different directions? You won't be able to go where I'm going if you're trying to hang with the in-crowd. Ya gotta pick one.*

But, if there are any others who are united in understanding of one's True Self, one can jam with those harmoniously, and it will be something else!

The line "Move mountains" in standard translations was also changed because it's so attached to our preconceptions. It's helpful to interpret this phrase without the pretext, but it's also significant that Jesus uses this in his analogy. To a Jew—his likely audience—it would not go unnoticed how mountains were very symbolic of places where God's Presence was undeniable. Mount Sinai, Mount Moriah, Mount Zion, Mount Ararat, and Mount Carmel all held huge meaning. It's reasonable that in its usage here, Jesus meant that one must recognize Oneness changes *where* Source is perceived, and that it's not bound to where it's expected—such as in powerful traditional places.

There may be some confusion in Saying 49, where many translate that there are those who "have been chosen." But in the Coptic, the stative verb here (ⲥⲟⲧⲡ̇) means "have chosen." If the author had wanted it to mean "have been chosen," it would read like it does in the next saying (ⲥⲱⲧⲡ̇). Just saying. Like we saw in Saying 23:

> "There's no special treatment for some, but punishment for others. There is only realizing that it's all One."

The Teacher is repeatedly intent on equality and "anti-specialness."

And when *the Teacher* brings up Light, it would have had a broad appeal in its time to everyone from Judaeans who embraced the Priestly sources of the Genesis creation account ("made in the image and likeness"), to Platonists (intelligence placed in a soul, and a soul in a body), to the Valentinians/gnostics (emanation), and proto-orthodoxy (especially Eastern and Syrian streams with the aspect of "theosis"). Yes, there is a Light.

If anyone asks, "Dude! Where's that beautiful music coming from?" Tell them. It's the song of Source, the rhythmic Light of Consciousness. Everyone (and everything) has a built–in tuner, too, so that you can stream it from anything, anywhere.

And when they say, "Oh yeah? Prove it!"

Just still yourself and listen! See? You can't stop yourself from swaying and dancing to the music.

Contemplative Reflection

How can we reconcile the idea that both a beginner and a seasoned spiritual practitioner can experience the same level of "Reality"? What does this suggest about the nature of spiritual understanding and the potential for sudden awakening?

This question challenges our assumptions about the linear progression of spiritual development. It prompts us to consider the possibility that profound insights can be accessed by anyone, regardless of their level of experience or knowledge.

What are the "two different paths" that *the Teacher* warns us against pursuing simultaneously? How can we ensure that our spiritual practices and beliefs are aligned and integrated, rather than fragmented and contradictory?

This question encourages us to reflect on the importance of focus and intentionality in our spiritual lives. It invites us to examine our own practices and beliefs to ensure that they are coherent and supportive of our overall spiritual goals.

Chapter 15 (Sayings 51 - 55)
Beyond Beliefs

51

The students asked, "When will those who have already died finally be able to rest in peace, and when will a New World come about?"

"Don't you get it?" said the Teacher, "All of that has already happened."

52

They continued asking questions. "You are the One that's been prophesied about all this time, right? An avatar or returning messiah, the next Buddha?"

The Teacher replied, "Why do you dismiss what I'm trying to teach you? Is it because I'm someone living, breathing and right in front of you? Are you saying that the dead have spoken to you, and told you something different?"

53

The students, again, asked, "So, what about religious practices that someone's parents offered for them? Is that any benefit?"

The Teacher replied, "Any benefit you have, you were already born with. Whatever it is that someone is trying to invoke in such rituals has already happened. It's only one's *own* understanding and intention that matter."

54

"It's best to be free from attachment, constriction, and distraction. Only from this freedom does one realize the Ultimate Reality of all things."

55

"You must set yourself free from 'this is what my parents believe,' and from what everyone around you is thinking or doing. Drink deeply from the Spring which gushes out from the

True Source. Get drunk on it. This is what I'm continually serving up for you.

"But if you can't accept this and you won't drink with me, then I'm wasting my time trying to convince you how we are equals, One and the same."

> (Standard Translation: Saying 51
> His disciples said to him, "When will the dead have rest, and when will the new world come?"
> He said to them, "What you're looking for has already come, but you don't know it."
>
> Saying 52
> His disciples said to him, "Twenty-four prophets have spoken in Israel, and they all spoke of you."
> He said to them, "You've ignored the Living One right in front of you, and you've talked about those who are dead."

Saying 53

His disciples said to him, "Is circumcision useful, or not?"

He said to them, "If it were useful, parents would have children who are born circumcised. But the true circumcision in spirit has become profitable in every way."

Saying 54

Jesus said, "Blessed are those who are poor, for yours is the kingdom of heaven."

Saying 55

Jesus said, "Whoever doesn't hate their father and mother can't become my disciple, and whoever doesn't hate their brothers and sisters and take up their cross like I do isn't worthy of me.")

What This Means

It isn't too long before one finds a string of questions by the students showing exactly how hard it is to step out of our comfort zone of indoctrination. What about fulfillment of

Biblical prophecies, about heaven, the afterlife, original sin, how one's parents' religious rituals get them a free pass—we still get these fears dumped all over us today, don't we?

Both the original and standard translations here have the disciples asking about circumcision—one of the practices that early Christian communities were also struggling with during the writings of Paul. But it could've been any tradition or ritual that puts reliance outside of our True Self.

(Interestingly, this is another point that lends to the Gospel of Thomas manuscript dating closer to the time of Paul, around 50 CE. It means the manuscript was likely written before this issue was resolved, that is, by the time the synoptic gospels were written between 65 & 130 CE.)

Spirit/ Christ/ Reality/ Kingdom or whatever one wishes to call it is right here and now, like it was before, and like it will always be. It has never belonged to just one exclusive group, and there have always been those who went before us who pointed the way to this understanding (and were often also ignored).

It is very easy to get locked into the traditions and practices of others we admire so that we seldom look at their meaning, their intention and usefulness. What we often get from them are their superstitions and habits of going through the motions of what one does or says in rote. *The Teacher* tries again to explain how the students must let go of all that to learn the teachings. Then, they can realize the equality and unity in both the death of ignorance and the rebirth into Awareness.

Contemplative Reflection

How can we recognize that the "New World" and the "rest in peace" we seek are already present, as *the Teacher* suggests? What might be preventing us from experiencing this reality in the here and now?

This question encourages us to reflect on our own beliefs about the afterlife and the possibility that the peace and renewal we long for are not distant or future states, but rather accessible in the present moment. It invites us to consider the ways in which our attachments, fears, and limiting beliefs may be obscuring our experience of this deeper reality.

What does *the Teacher's* response to the question about religious practices reveal about the relationship between external rituals and inner intention? How can we cultivate a spiritual practice that is grounded in genuine inner intention, rather than blind adherence to tradition?

This question challenges us to examine our own motivations for engaging in spiritual practices. It prompts us to consider whether our actions are driven by a genuine desire for connection and understanding, or by a sense of obligation or fear. It encourages us to cultivate a spiritual practice that is authentic, meaningful, and aligned with our deepest values and aspirations.

Chapter 16 (Sayings 56 - 59)
Beyond the Struggling

56

"One who has stumbled across the facts about this world *as it truly is*, understands that it's only a container, a vehicle to get them where they're going, a body without life on its own. There's nothing one owes to their corpse."

57

"Consciousness is like a gardener who has a good, viable seed. When a rival who opposes the gardener sneaks into his garden at night, they plant a seemingly similar seed there that is toxic. The gardener can tell when this happens but won't allow his helpers to pull it up, as their healthy seedling might be removed or damaged, too. They will wait until harvest, when it's obvious, and then the poisonous plant will be yanked out and destroyed."

58

"Even though it may not seem so at the time, the struggles one faces and makes the effort to overcome are worth it. These are the living encounters within non-dual Reality."

59

"Pay close attention to the Living Oneness. That way you won't face death oblivious to what you're really looking at."

(Standard Translation: Saying 56
Jesus said, "Whoever has known the world has found a corpse. Whoever has found a corpse, of them the world isn't worthy."

Saying 57
Jesus said, "My Fathers' kingdom can be compared to someone who had good seed. Their enemy came by night and sowed weeds among the good seed. The person didn't let anyone pull out the weeds, 'so that you don't pull out the wheat along with the weeds,' they said to them. 'On the day of the harvest,

the weeds will be obvious. Then they'll be pulled out and burned.' "

Saying 58
Jesus said, "Blessed is the person who's gone to a lot of trouble. They've found life."

Saying 59
Jesus said, "Look for the Living One while you're still alive. If you die and then try to look for him, you won't be able to.")

What This Means

The conversation continues by showing how illusion and ignorance are not the counterbalance to Awareness. All beliefs are not "basically the same." It's just that there's no substance in them to assign value or weight. Throughout the text, *the Teacher* references "the world," "a corpse," or "the body." It's helpful to understand that the context here continues with that earlier notion of *going through the motions.* There's no point to living in our bodies without regard for our soul.

On the day of harvest, the weeds will be obvious. There's an interesting lesson about the weeds the rival sows. It's sometimes translated as *tares*, or *darnel*, which is a crop that looks like wheat at first. It grows under the same conditions, too, but the bread made with it causes hallucinations. If these are mixed in, one will see things that aren't there.

The Teacher is quick to point out that making the effort to take the right path is tough but worthwhile. It's ultimately the only way to be Alive while you're living.

Contemplative Reflection

What does *the Teacher* mean when they say the world is "a body without life on its own"? How can we reconcile our experience of the physical world with the idea that it is ultimately incomplete or a temporary vessel?

This question encourages us to explore the deeper nature of reality and to question our assumptions about the material world. It prompts us to consider the possibility that there is a more fundamental reality beyond the physical senses.

How does the parable of the gardener and the toxic seed relate to our own spiritual journey? What are the "toxic seeds" that may be planted in our minds or hearts, and how can we cultivate discernment and patience in order to distinguish them from the "good seed"?

This question invites us to reflect on the challenges of spiritual growth and the potential for deception or confusion. It encourages us to cultivate mindfulness and discernment in order to navigate these challenges and stay on the path of truth.

Chapter 17 (Sayings 60 - 62)
Duality, Darkness, and Deeper

60

"Did you see the man at the market who was holding a small animal cage?" asked the Teacher, "The animal belongs to him now."

"I bet he's going to kill and eat it," said the students.

The Teacher replied, "As long as it's alive, he won't. He must kill and cook it first."

His students said, "Well sure. He'd get sick and could even die if he just ate it raw."

"You should find a place for repose, so you, too, don't just end up on someone else's plate," said the Teacher.

61

"There are two sprawled across a couch. One will die, the other will live."

The Welcoming Friend said, "Which one are you, coming over here and stretching out on my couch, even after eating at my table?"

The Teacher said, "I am from the One, which makes all of us equals. This is what Consciousness has me doing now.

The Welcoming Friend replied, "It's because I am from the One that I, too, can say, 'When one is empty, they will be filled with Light, but if one is divided, darkness fills their belly.' "

62

"I'm happy to explain these deeper things, but only with those who know their value. Here we can see it, how one's left and right hands do not need to explain what the other is doing in order to understand."

(Standard Translation: Saying 60

They saw a Samaritan carrying a lamb to Judea. He said to his disciples, "What do you think he's going to do with that lamb?"

They said to him, "He's going to kill it and eat it."

He said to them, "While it's living, he won't eat it, but only after he kills it and it becomes a corpse."

They said, "He can't do it any other way."

He said to them, "You, too, look for a resting place, so that you won't become a corpse and be eaten."

Saying 61: Jesus and Salome

Jesus said, "Two will rest on a couch. One will die, the other will live."

Salome said, "Who are you, Sir, to climb onto my couch and eat off my table as if you're from someone?"

Jesus said to her, "I'm the one who exists in equality. Some of what belongs to my Father was given to me."

"I'm your disciple."

"So I'm telling you, if someone is equal, they'll be full of light; but if they're divided, they'll be full of darkness."

Saying 62
Jesus said, "I tell my mysteries to those who are worthy of my mysteries. Don't let your left hand know what your right hand is doing.")

What This Means

This section begins with *the Teacher* and his students seemingly heading to a dinner with friends. In standard translations (and original texts, for that matter) it began with Jesus and the disciples en route to Judea. It continues with the gang gathering with friends.

Surely his students aren't really being asked about what a customer in the checkout line might have been thinking about for dinner. Instead, it's a subtle lesson to see if they notice how they might find themselves in society's cage. Not a safe place to be if one was hoping to remain a free range, living soul. But on the menu tonight, False Self is the main course, with a savory side of ego. Yum!

I guess when they got to the party *the Teacher* decided it needed a little livening up, maybe grabbed their glass and spoon. *Ding ding ding!* Ah hem. *Two are reclining on the couch; One's gonna live, the other's gonna die.*

"Whoa! Did you invite this guy? Say something before anyone else gets spooked!"

"Beg your pardon, dude, you're right here eating my grub and chilling with me on the sofa. What the hell, man."
The host in the standard translation is named Salome. We know of a Salome who was a friend and follower of Jesus mentioned in the Gospel of Mark. It's a beautiful name meaning "peace" and it's no surprise that someone like her

would graciously offer her sofa and a meal with anyone.

She is actually mentioned in several extra-canonical texts, such as *Pistis Sophia, Contra Celsum, Apocalypse of James, Book of Bartholomew, Psalms of Heracleides, Kephalaia,* and others. In each, she stands tall and strong and understands fully, just like our *Tower.*

When we see *the Teacher* answer with exactly who he is, the Welcoming Friend shows who she is, in like awareness. It's a powerful response that's echoed in the Manichaean Psalms of Thomas (16), where she exclaims:

> "Jesus, may you hear me, for I am not in doubt. One is my heart, one is my thinking, no thought in my heart is split or diverged."

The Teacher then shares how these mysteries are not revealed to just anyone, but only to those who are ready to understand them or "listens with their Heart" as in Saying 24. For those who do understand, even if they seem separate or opposites—like a left and right hand—they are connected and aware, without any need to control or be nosy.

Whew. Nice save. In fact, it's so nice that right now looks like a good time for a couple of cool stories. There's three more tucked away in my pocket...

Contemplative Reflection

What is the deeper meaning of *the Teacher's* statement, "You should find a place for repose, so you, too, don't just end up on someone else's plate"? How does this relate to the themes of spiritual awakening and self-realization?

This question prompts reflection on the metaphorical language used by the Teacher. It encourages us to consider the potential consequences of remaining spiritually "uncooked" or unaware, and the importance of seeking a state of inner peace and understanding.

How does *the Teacher's* interaction with *the Welcoming Friend* illustrate the principles of equality and interconnectedness? What can we learn from this exchange about the nature of true spiritual friendship and the dissolution of egoic boundaries?

This question invites us to examine the dynamics of the conversation between the Teacher and the Welcoming Friend. It encourages us to consider how spiritual awareness can lead to a sense of oneness and interconnectedness with others, and how this can transform our relationships and interactions.

Chapter 18 (Sayings 63 - 65)
The Traps of the Transactional

63

"Imagine a wealthy man who has a lot of resources. 'I'm going to take my funds and invest them and profit even more, and invest that, too, making billions!' It consumes his thoughts and drives his desires—right up until his death that night.

"Do you get what I'm saying?"

64

"Imagine a woman who has decided to host a party for her friends. She started to prepare dinner and plan activities when she asked her roommate if she could help confirm everyone who was coming.

"Her roommate reached out to the first friend. 'Hey, just making sure you're still coming tonight.'

"'I can't,' they said, 'some business partners owe me money, and they're swinging by tonight. I've got to wait around here so I can get paid. Sorry.'

"The roommate reached out to the next friend. 'Hey, just making sure you're still coming tonight.'

"'I can't,' they said, 'contractors are coming to my new house, and after meeting with them, I don't know if I'll have any time. Sorry.'

"Her roommate reached out to another friend. 'Hey, just making sure you're still coming tonight.'

"'I'd love to, but I can't,' they said, 'I have another friend who's getting married soon, and I was asked to set up the catering for them. Sorry.'

"Again, the roommate reached out to more friends. 'Hey, just making sure you're still coming tonight.'

"'Wish we could, but we can't,' they said, 'we came into this real estate deal, and we're going over to pick up the rent. Sorry.'

"The roommate returned and told her, 'Everyone on your list has these excuses and can't come after all.'

"By now, the woman was nearly finished with all the preparations. 'What? Then please, just go out and invite our neighbors, or strangers for all I care. Whoever wants to come.'

"Consciousness is not about transactions. There's no business to be done with it."

65

"There once lived a man who was a winemaker. I'm not saying he was a lazy winemaker, but I'm not saying he wasn't either.

"You see, instead of working the vineyards himself or hiring workers, he decided to make a little extra money by leasing it to some farmers.

"One day, he sent one of his workers to collect the grapes they had picked. The farmers were furious and beat him up, badly.

"The worker returned and told his boss.

"'Guess they didn't recognize that he was one of my guys,' the winemaker said, 'I'll send someone who they know who works for me.'

"The farmers beat him up, as well.

"The winemaker was shocked. 'Surely, they'll show respect to my own son. We were all there together when they signed the lease.'

"The farmers quickly grabbed and killed him, because they knew he was the winemaker's heir to the vineyards.

"Listen closely to what I've told you. Try to understand what all this really means."

> (Standard Translation: Saying 63
> Jesus said, "There was a rich man who had much money. He said, 'I'll use my money to sow, reap, plant, and fill my barns with fruit, so that I won't need anything.' That's what he was thinking to himself, but he died that very night. Anyone who has ears to hear should hear!"

Saying 64

Jesus said, "Someone was planning on having guests. When dinner was ready, they sent their servant to call the visitors.

"The servant went to the first and said, 'My master invites you.'

"They said, 'Some merchants owe me money. They're coming tonight. I need to go and give them instructions. Excuse me from the dinner.'

"The servant went to another one and said, 'My master invites you.'

"They said, "I've just bought a house and am needed for the day. I won't have time.'

"The servant went to another one and said, 'My master invites you.'

"They said, 'My friend is getting married and I'm going to make dinner. I can't come. Excuse me from the dinner.'

"The servant went to another one and said, 'My master invites you.'

"They said, "I've just bought a farm and am going to collect the rent. I can't come. Excuse me.'

"The servant went back and told the master, 'The ones you've invited to the dinner have excused themselves.'

"The master said to their servant, 'Go out to the roads and bring whomever you find so that they can have dinner.'

"Buyers and merchants won't enter the places of my Father."

Saying 65

He said, "A creditor owned a vineyard. He leased it out to some sharecroppers to work it so he could collect its fruit.

"He sent his servant so that the sharecroppers could give him the fruit of the vineyard. They seized his servant, beat him, and nearly killed him.

"The servant went back and told his master. His master said, 'Maybe he just didn't know them.' He sent another servant, but the tenants beat that one too.

"Then the master sent his son, thinking, 'Maybe they'll show some respect to my son.'

"Because they knew that he was the heir of the vineyard, the sharecroppers seized and killed him. Anyone who has ears to hear should hear!")

What This Means

The first story makes the urgent point that we need to do what we can when we can. I can go along with that. You?

The next one is a little longer, but still a good one. It's a nice reminder: Be hospitable; but when you are a host of others, realize that some of the people you think of as friends will make excuses, while *you* are the one making all the effort.

But let's not just waive off a good celebration. No way. Through the gospels as well, we find Jesus at several festivities and dinners. There's something wonderful about those who we might think of as friends or "chosen families." This recognition recurs throughout the text, too.

It's also fair to look at the story from the perspective of the friend/guest, that we should be a good and grateful one.

I should mention that as we read these texts, there are different ways that they can speak to us. It's important to recognize that they are written by a person, for a particular person or group, in a specific cultural context, but the Source is living. These stories can show you and me meanings in a myriad of ways.

This parable, for example, recently had me reflecting on the "invited guests" as my own beliefs and behaviors. I thought some of them were close to me and served me back as I devoted myself to and served them. But when I faced a personal crisis, and I turned to them needing them to rally behind me and as allies by my side, they had excuses for not showing up. In the same way, too, I found solidarity and eventually celebration with strangers who showed. What I learned from this parable wasn't necessarily the author's intention, nor was I the intended audience, and I hardly came close to sharing its cultural context. But it spoke deeply to me, and who am I to limit Spirit? Free from distortion, expectation or projection, the music was great, and the party was something I won't forget.

Back to the text. The last story may come off as a bit of a buzzkill, but it is still a great lesson. Here, one finds a person who's well off enough to have their own wine vineyard. Nice, right? Who wouldn't love that? But one has to wonder about this next part: Let's see... They're too lazy to do any of the work themselves and too greedy not to hire workers. So, what do they do? They lease the land out—and *then* expect to take the crop!

The story does not justify the reaction of the sharecroppers. Murdering is bad, but that's not the point. This one is another example of how self-serving actions and attitudes of an imperial, even religious, society have devastating consequences. Metaphorically, the vineyard is the owner's responsibility to attend and cultivate, to grow and harvest, to take and let ferment, and to eventually enjoy and share with others, before sowing again.

(One can picture everybody nodding *Right On!* At least one hopes so because it looks like there's more to say about it...)

Contemplative Reflection

What is the message behind the parable of the rich man who dies before enjoying his wealth? How does this parable relate to *the Teacher's* emphasis on spiritual awareness and the impermanence of material possessions?

This question encourages reflection on the parable's message about the futility of chasing material wealth at the expense of spiritual fulfillment. It prompts us to consider how we can prioritize what truly matters in life.

What lessons can we learn from the parable of the woman hosting a party and the excuses of her invited guests? How does this parable relate to *the Teacher's* teachings about the importance of prioritizing spiritual connection and the challenges of navigating worldly distractions?

This question invites us to examine the parable's message about the distractions and excuses that can prevent us from engaging in meaningful connection. It encourages us to reflect on how we can prioritize spiritual community and overcome the obstacles that may hinder our participation.

What does the story about the winemaker intend to teach us about doing the "hard work?" What does it teach us about social responsibility? How is justice and spiritual development intertwined with it?

This question has us considering the parable's message about both our spiritual and social duties. It shows us the connections between commitment and concern and fairness.

Chapter 19 (Sayings 66 - 71)
The Haughty, the Hated, the Head and the Heart

66

"What do you think that religious experts, scholars, celebrities or specialists say about Ultimate Reality? They typically deny that there's any proof of it. But in truth, it's what the entirety of existence is built from."

67

"Those who 'know everything' but nothing about their own Oneness, lack everything worth knowing."

68

"Rest assured. Even those who are hated and bullied will find happiness. Their aggressors can try to reach the True Self, but they will still never get close."

69

"Those who have searched for their True Self are so very lucky. They know Oneness and will be completely filled after hungering for it for so long."

70

"When you bring out that which is from inside your True Self, this is what will sustain you. But if you don't have it, how can you bring it out? So, that will be the thing that kills you."

71

"I'm going to destroy this mental model of where we think we live. I'll condemn it like an abandoned building, leveling it to the ground so no one can rebuild it."

> (Standard Translation: Saying 66
> Jesus said, "Show me the stone the builders rejected; that's the cornerstone."

Saying 67

Jesus said, "Whoever knows everything, but is personally lacking, lacks everything."

Saying 68

Jesus said, "Blessed are you when you're hated and persecuted, and no place will be found where you've been persecuted."

Saying 69

Jesus said, "Blessed are those who've been persecuted in their own hearts. They've truly known the Father. Blessed are those who are hungry, so that their stomachs may be filled."

Saying 70

Jesus said, "If you give birth to what's within you, what you have within you will save you. If you don't have that within you, what you don't have within you will kill you."

Saying 71

Jesus said, "I'll destroy this house, and no one will be able to build it ...")

What This Means

One can assume *the Teacher* still has everyone's attention. *Scoot in a bit. I've got more.* His friends may perhaps be wondering whose side of the line (a line they never drew but was drawn for them) they are on.

Society has plenty of self-appointed experts on everything. And what is it that they say about Ultimate Reality? They just keep claiming how *it's this* or *it's that* or *there's no such thing.* We see this all over the media nowadays, too, don't we? However, Source is what the entire universe is built of and upon. And if one doesn't know that, what good is anything they know?

People might tease or disparage us for recognizing our True Self, but the True Self— which fulfills and sustains us—is something those people cannot reach. Yet, society's ideologies are not satisfying or life-giving. They are illusions that say these carefully decorated sandcastles are real palaces.

Saying 71 has several parallels. Matt 24:1 & 2, Matt 26:59-68, Matt 27:39-40, John 2:13-22, Mark 14:55-65, Mark 15:29-30, Mark 13:1-4, Acts 6:12-14 to name a few. In Matthew, for example, this follows his harsh rebuke of the scribes and Pharisees in a list of woes. Then he laments over Jerusalem.

And what do his disciples do when Jesus walks out? "Say, have you noticed the craftsmanship of these temple complexes? They're really something else, aren't they!"

It's the man-made constructs, the ideologies that he's talking about destroying. And IYKYK. (If You Know, You Know.)

Contemplative Reflection

How can we recognize and connect with the "Ultimate Reality" that *the Teacher* claims is the foundation of existence, even in the face of skepticism from experts and authorities?

This question encourages us to explore our own understanding of reality and to question the prevailing narratives presented by those in positions of power. It invites us to seek a deeper truth that transcends conventional knowledge and beliefs.

What does *the Teacher* mean by "destroying this mental model of where we think we live"? How might this relate to the process of spiritual awakening and the dismantling of our preconceived notions about ourselves and the world?

This question prompts us to examine our own mental constructs and belief systems. It challenges us to consider how these constructs might be limiting our understanding of reality and preventing us from experiencing a more expansive and liberated state of being.

Chapter 20 (Sayings 72 - 75)
Separate or Seeking

72

Someone approached the Teacher and said, "You've got to tell my siblings that they have to share our family inheritance with me."

The Teacher responded, "Hold on. Who made me the Great Divider: one to portion out possessions?"

Turning to the students, the Teacher asked, "Am I the kind of person who does another's work for them? Do I ever take One and break it apart into shards and fragments?"

73

"Many out there are starving for Awareness. The crop is massive, but there are hardly any workers. Go and beg the harvest boss to dispatch more workers to the fields."

74

"There are so many people who are looking for a connection. Their heads are spinning from their separation from Source, but nobody admits it's making them sick."

75

"Large crowds are simply standing outside the door of Awareness, but only One is going in."

(Standard Translation: Saying 72
Someone said to him, "Tell my brothers to divide our inheritance with me."
He said to him, "Who made me a divider?"
He turned to his disciples and said to them, "Am I really a divider?"

Saying 73
Jesus said, "The harvest really is plentiful, but the workers are few. So pray that the Lord will send workers to the harvest."
Saying 74
He said, "Lord, many are gathered around the well, but there's nothing to drink."

Saying 75

Jesus said, "Many are waiting at the door, but those who are one will enter the bridal chamber.")

What This Means

This conversation may not have happened while still at their friend's place, but it tracks with what *the Teacher* has been saying. Either way, someone approached, hoping he would take their side, and their problem would be fixed. *Oh man, more line drawers. Didn't we just talk about a guy with the vineyard, pawning off the work that they needed to do for themselves?*

The Teacher shares how much is ripe for the picking and needed for all the hunger in the world. Hardly just metaphoric, even today. As well, *the Teacher* tells them that society leaves one with a false sense of belonging, but no one wants to admit it. "Fake it 'til ya make it" is terrible spiritual advice.

Most translations miss the mark a little here in Saying 74, about "nothing to drink from the well." Aside from scholars Linssen, Grondin, Wolfe, and Koepke, everyone else has just lined up behind the translator Guillaumont's changing of the original text. He matched it to something from Origen's attribution to a missing or made-up piece against Celsus. But this is not what the text says. It would be like all of the translators of the Bible accepting someone's changes to John 3:16 as *"For God so loved Chicago so much that he sent his only son, and whoever believes in him shall get deep dish pizza."* No doubt, God does love Chicago, and one should try Chicago–style pizza, but that's not the text either.

At least Gathercole notes:

> The two sources of water have both been subjects of discussion: the text has x ⲱⲧⲉ ('penetration, separation') and ⳉ ⲱⲛⲉ ('sickness'), neither of which make good sense. Proposed as alternatives are ⳉ ⲱⲧⲉ

('well, cistern, pit', Crum 595a) and ϭ ⲱⲧ ('drinking trough', Crum 833a; var. ϫ ⲱⲧ B). Most editors propose emending ⲱ ⲱⲛⲉ at the end to ⲱ ⲱⲧⲉ. More diverse has been opinion about the earlier ϫ ⲱⲧⲉ, seen by Layton as a variation of ϭ ⲱⲧ (hence Lambdin's translation 'drinking trough') but by Plisch as a variant of ⲱ ⲱⲧⲉ (translated, 'well').

Sadly, he stops there. And that's *really* disappointing, because healing the sick is primary to Jesus's agenda. So, let's go with the original text's correct translation. Agreed?

There's an urgency *the Teacher* keeps referencing (as in Saying 21, to eat the fruit while it's still ripe), and the healing is found only within the interior, where the Awareness of the One is. You can't just stand outside, waiting on the surface.

Contemplative Reflection

How does *the Teacher's* response to the visitors' inheritance dispute challenge our expectations of how a spiritual leader should act? What does this reveal about *the Teacher's* emphasis on personal responsibility and inner work?

This question encourages us to reflect on the Teacher's reluctance to intervene in worldly affairs. It prompts us to consider how his teachings emphasize individual agency and inner transformation, rather than relying on external authorities to solve our problems.

What is the significance of *the Teacher's* call for more "workers" in Saying 73? How does this relate to the idea that there is a "hunger" for spiritual awareness in the world, and what responsibility do we have to address this need?

This question invites us to consider our own role in spreading spiritual awareness and contributing to the well-being of others. It prompts us to reflect on how we can actively participate in the "harvest" of souls and help others find their way back to Source.

Chapter 21 (Sayings 76 - 81)
Beyond Materiality

76

The Teacher said, "A marketplace vendor had a booth full of merchandise. Upon seeing another with a single, most beautiful pearl, he wisely sold everything he had—merchandise, tent, displays, equipment, all of it—just to buy the pearl. You should be the same as the vendor. Seek out that which is eternal, incorruptible, invaluable, and beautiful."

77

Speaking as Source, the Teacher added, "I am Light, shining over everything manifested, in it and through it. Everything comes from me, and everything flows back to me. Chop and split a chunk of wood, and you will see that I have embodied it. Look to see what's hiding under a rock, and I am there, too."

78

"Why have you come outside and gather into a crowd, waiting for something? Is it to hear some famous speaker blow hot air? Sure, they may dress the part, like they're someone important or gifted, but they haven't the slightest clue about Truth."

79

A woman from the crowd came up to the Teacher. "Your mother is so lucky to have given birth to and nourished you."

"Those who have understood the call of Consciousness, nurturing and looking after it, are the truly lucky ones," replied the Teacher, "You know, there may come a time for one to say, 'Wow. They're so lucky that they *don't* have any kids.'"

80

"Once you have begun to understand the material world, no doubt you've discovered this physical body. You also know the world holds no scale for determining what's valuable, even with regards to our bodies."

81

"Let the one who has understood Real Value take control of the All. Let those who know their True power melt into this stillness and bliss."

(Standard Translation: Saying 76
Jesus said, "The Father's kingdom can be compared to a merchant with merchandise who found a pearl. The merchant was wise; they sold their merchandise and bought that single pearl for themselves.
"You, too, look for the treasure that doesn't perish but endures, where no moths come to eat and no worms destroy."

Saying 77
Jesus said, "I'm the light that's over all. I am the All. The All has come from me and unfolds toward me.
"Split a log; I'm there. Lift the stone, and you'll find me there."

Saying 78

Jesus said, "What did you go out into the desert to see? A reed shaken by the wind? A person wearing fancy clothes, like your rulers and powerful people? They wear fancy clothes, but can't know the truth."

Saying 79

A woman in the crowd said to him, "Blessed is the womb that bore you, and the breasts that nourished you."

He said to her, "Blessed are those who have listened to the message of the Father and kept it, because there will be days when you'll say, 'Blessed is the womb that didn't conceive and the breasts that haven't given milk.' "

Saying 80

Jesus said, "Whoever has known the world has found the body; but whoever has found the body, of them the world isn't worthy."

Saying 81

Jesus said, "Whoever has become rich should become a ruler, and whoever has power should renounce it.")

What This Means

The Teacher and the students may have left the party by this point. Perhaps they were even passing through the same market along the way where they saw the guy with a caged animal, and it wouldn't be a stretch to imagine it next to a coast where people are gathered.

Was it time for another quick lesson, maybe a spin on the ol' big fish story? Awareness is invaluable and greater when compared with all this small stuff on the surface. *Let it all go and get yourself that pearl.*

The Teacher may have found a crowd gathering around. This really would not have been so unusual. *I am—and you are—from the Light, return to the Light, and in fact am/are the Light. The Light of Consciousness that embodies all materiality and all that is hidden or immaterial.* Slight spoiler alert: this concept is broken down right off the bat in Mary's Gospel that follows this Thomas text, too. Okay, that's all I'm saying about that here, but Saying 77 is a beautiful concept that we find in many more places than just inside wood and under rocks.

Psalm 139:7-8 says, "Where can I go to escape Your Spirit? Where can I flee from Your presence? If I ascend to the heavens, You are there; if I make my bed in Sheol, You are there." (Berean Standard Bible)

In the Bhagavad Gita 4.24, we read:

ब्रह्मार्पणं ब्रह्म हविर्ब्रह्माग्नौ ब्रह्मणा हुतम् ।

ब्रह्मैव तेन गन्तव्यं ब्रह्मकर्मसमाधिना ॥

brahmārpaṇaṁ brahma havir
brahmāgnau brahmaṇā hutam
brahmaiva tena gantavyaṁ brahma-karma-
samādhinā

Meaning this, "For those who are completely absorbed in God-consciousness, the oblation is Brahman (Ultimate Reality), the ladle with which it is offered is Brahman, the act of offering is Brahman, and the sacrificial fire is also Brahman. Such persons, who view everything as God, easily attain Him."

Most translations of the Gospel of Thomas Saying 78 also have Jesus asking what people were doing out there, "Watching the reeds blow in the wind?" This is likely a jab at Herod Antipas, the ruler of the region who opposed John the Baptist and Jesus.

Antipas at the time was preening for the emperor by building, then moving his capital from Sepphoris—which was an area that Jesus and John would have frequented, and Nazareth was a suburb of—to Tiberias, right on the coast of the Sea of Galilee (ergo the reeds blowing in the wind). Why in the world would Antipas do this? It was to dominate commerce and wealth throughout the region. This move was without doubt one that squeezed the livelihoods of most

Judaeans and Galileans, causing a great deal of extra suffering to the people there.

Don't pay any attention to charlatans who simply put on a show. It's all smoke and mirrors, folks. A flaunt and power trip. Hang around and I'll tell ya how you can discover the Real Deal.

When an onlooker tries to sing his praises, *the Teacher* redirects the praise towards those who recognize Consciousness. Their eyes are on Source, not on being highly recognized or making clones of themselves.

Society is simply a man-made construct, all about power and creating minions to serve itself. Once this becomes clear, one knows the Value of Nature and the cheapness of fabricated stuff.

The standard translation of Saying 81 sounds tricky at first: "Let the rich be king, and let the powerful denounce it?" I really think this aphorism follows what is explained as the True Value inferred right before it. It also connects back to the bit in Saying 2 where one is seeking, struggling, wondering, discovering and "reigning over the all" to then find "stillness and repose." It also ties in nicely with Saying 7 about nature's strength and freedom, *but not dominance.* The teacher just spoke about the fake values of kings and celebrities in Saying 78, leading quite nicely into the next part, in Saying 82. But you can pocket that for now. We'll get there soon enough.

Contemplative Reflection

What is the "single, most beautiful pearl" that *the Teacher* encourages us to seek? How can we prioritize this eternal treasure over the temporary allure of material possessions and worldly pursuits?

This question prompts us to reflect on our values and priorities. It challenges us to consider what truly matters in life and how we can align our actions with our deepest aspirations.

How can we cultivate a deeper awareness of the Light of Consciousness that *the Teacher* describes as being present in all things? What practices or perspectives might help us recognize and connect with this Divine presence in our everyday lives?

This question encourages us to explore the interconnectedness of all things and to seek a more profound understanding of the Divine presence within ourselves and the world around us. It invites us to cultivate a sense of awe and wonder in the face of creation.

Chapter 22 (Sayings 82 - 84)
Beyond Form

82

"If you are close to me, you are close to this inner flame. There are those who think I'm just 'way out there,' too far off to possibly be right, and that's fine. But it means they're distant from Awareness."

83

"Images manifest, appearing from within people, but the Light that's inside of them is hidden by the Light of Awareness. It will be revealed, but beyond figure and form, it stays obscured by its Light."

84

"Now, when you see your own likeness, as when you're looking at a mirror, you're happy, right? But once you perceive your True Image— which has been there long before you and can't become visible or die off—it can really feel like more than you can handle."

(Standard Translation: Saying 82
Jesus said, "Whoever is near me is near the fire, and whoever is far from me is far from the kingdom."

Saying 83
Jesus said, "Images are revealed to people, but the light within them is hidden in the image of the Father's light. He'll be revealed, but his image will be hidden by his light."

Saying 84
Jesus said, "When you see your likeness, you rejoice. But when you see your images that came into being before you did – which don't die, and aren't revealed – how much you'll have to bear!")

What This Means

Here, we touch on Fire again. It's the Fire he brings to the world. The Fire that's tended until it catches flame. The Fire that causes the Spring to bubble forth from Source. The Fire that burns away misconceptions. The Fire that brings Light. The Light of Awareness. The Light of Consciousness. The Light that is emitted through the Heart, to shine on the Path, to fill dark, empty spaces. The Light that flows to and from Source, reflecting and revealing everything deeply perceivable while blinding everything viewed with our basic five senses.

All of this really is absolutely more than one can possibly handle. To me, it sounds a lot like Saying 50, "Where the Light of Consciousness expresses itself, even as everything that we perceive." And I'm here for it! Are you seeing, too, how well all of this flows together?

Contemplative Reflection

What is the relationship between the "inner flame" and "Awareness" that *the Teacher* speaks of? How can we cultivate a closer proximity to this inner flame in order to expand our awareness and understanding?

This question prompts us to explore the connection between our inner fire, or Presence, and our capacity for spiritual awareness. It encourages us to consider practices that might kindle this inner flame and lead to a deeper understanding of ourselves and the world around us.

How does the concept of the "True Image" that exists beyond form and visibility challenge our conventional understanding of identity and selfhood? In what ways might encountering this True Image be both overwhelming and liberating?

This question invites us to contemplate the nature of our true identity and to consider the possibility that it transcends our physical form and personality. It encourages us to explore the potential for a deeper and more expansive sense of self that can be both awe-inspiring and transformative.

Chapter 23 (Sayings 85 - 90)
The Call of Consciousness

85

"Stories such as how the Big Bang occurred, or the beginning of life, or the 'seven days of creation' can sound so incredible! Yet the realization of your own Oneness is honestly greater. Even Adam would be jealous to understand it for himself, and to not face the death."

86

"Those who are concerned with material things can at best only find slight comfort in life. It's the same with those whose heads are in the clouds and hopes in a heaven, too. But it can be hard to feel comfortable in one's own skin, trying to both live as a human being while also trying to live into this Awareness."

87

"A person will be miserable, having to depend merely on another person. Their soul, too, if it has to have an *other*."

88

"Consciousness is sending you a message. It's a free offer that can be redeemed for your True Self. Now, it's up to you to release the false *sense* of Self, asking, 'When would you like to come get this imposter? It's all yours.' "

89

"Do you only wash the outside of your cup? Why is its appearance so important? Who you are matters so much more than just how you seem."

90

Speaking as the One, the Teacher said, "Come over here. I can help with your heavy load. I can help make your journey a lot easier, and you can finally settle into your rhythm."

(Standard Translation: Saying 85
Jesus said, "Adam came into being from a great power and great wealth, but he didn't become worthy of you. If he had been worthy, he wouldn't have tasted death."

Saying 86
Jesus said, "The foxes have dens and the birds have nests, but the Son of Humanity has nowhere to lay his head and rest."

Saying 87
Jesus said, "How miserable is the body that depends on a body, and how miserable is the soul that depends on both."

Saying 88
Jesus said, "The angels and the prophets will come to you and give you what belongs to you. You'll give them what you have and ask yourselves, 'When will they come and take what is theirs?'"

Saying 89
Jesus said, "Why do you wash the outside of the cup? Don't you know that whoever created the inside created the outside too?"

Saying 90

Jesus said, "Come to me, because my yoke is easy and my requirements are light. You'll be refreshed.")

What This Means

The Teacher is again bragging about those who understand their connection to Consciousness. Early he brings up his own teacher, now it is with Adam, the first human—*and you're right there, up at that level.*

Sure, it's a peace that surpasses financial security or religious practices, or anything. But this level of Awareness isn't always warm and cozy. Our "suits of skin" can feel a bit itchy sometimes, huh.

The Teacher also asks, *Dude! What's with the clean looking cup that's still super nasty inside? You're not gonna drink from that, are ya?* It has parallels in both Matthew and Luke where he's

193

blasting Pharisees for their hypocrisy. I mean, think about it. That stuff we don't purge leaves a stain. And not just that, but like bacteria it grows fuzzy, and not it a cute and cuddly way.

Just being a human can be difficult, as it sometimes forces a dependency on others. It's harder when it seems like our True Self is counting on our body, and harder still when it must count on another person other than ourselves for everything. One must give it the proper attention. *And I can help you with this.*

Contemplative Reflection

How can we reconcile the challenges of living in the material world with the pursuit of spiritual awareness? How can we find a balance between our human experience and our yearning for a deeper connection to Consciousness?

This question prompts us to explore the tension between our embodied existence and our spiritual aspirations. It encourages us to seek a way to integrate these seemingly disparate aspects of ourselves.

What does *the Teacher* mean by the statement, "Consciousness is sending you a message"? How can we become more receptive to these messages and open ourselves to the possibility of reclaiming our True Self?

This question invites us to consider the ways in which Consciousness might be communicating with us, perhaps through intuition, synchronicity, or other subtle cues. It encourages us to cultivate a sense of openness and receptivity in order to receive these messages and embark on the journey of self-discovery.

Chapter 24 (Sayings 91 - 95)
Beyond the Surface

91

A group of people asked, "Who are you? Tell us, so we can believe what you're saying."

The Teacher said, "You scrutinize everything, don't you, whether it's religion, science, politics. Right now, you need to recognize what's right in front of you, and how critical of a time it is to understand it."

92

"If you search deeply, you'll find it. In the past, when you were inquiring about things, I couldn't go very deeply into it. It would've been too much. Even now, I am willing to explain it all, but you're still not seriously interested."

93

"No one should give their own deep Truths to those who aren't interested or paying close attention. Might as well give that pearl to a pet that would drag it out into the yard, or a farm animal that would just trample and crush it."

94

"Again, if you search deeply, you'll find it. The door won't be opened unless you're first knocking."

95

"As far as resources go, however, one who has plenty should not go around lending and charging interest. It's much better to give it away to someone in need, without reimbursement or expectations."

(Standard Translation: Saying 91
They said to him, "Tell us who you are so that we may trust you."

He said to them, "You read the face of the sky and the earth, but you don't know the one right in front of you, and you don't know how to read the present moment."

Saying 92

Jesus said, "Look and you'll find. I didn't answer your questions before. Now I want to give you answers, but you aren't looking for them."

Saying 93

"Don't give what's holy to the dogs, or else it might be thrown on the manure pile. Don't throw pearls to the pigs, or else they might ..."

Saying 94

Jesus said, "Whoever looks will find, and whoever knocks, it will be opened for them."

Saying 95

Jesus said, "If you have money, don't lend it at interest. Instead, give it to someone from whom you won't get it back.")

What This Means

Here, the crowd is really listening up. It could be that at least some have listened to him before. *"Tell us who you are again? We like your stuff, but it lands a little differently than the churches in town."* No doubt, within the crowd of people, not everyone had the exact same worldview. It's likely there was a mix of class and gender and race, with some in every crowd that were there to be healed or see a healing, some looking for their own hero to step up and free them from their oppressors, and some who may have felt threatened by and challenged these teachings.

Go deep. Listen with your heart. Here's your answer. I can imagine *the Teacher* turning towards his students. *Do you guys still have those pearls? Don't just go showing them off to folks who don't understand their value.*

The Teacher encourages everyone to keep seeking—not *the Teacher*, not any affiliation, but Consciousness. The path is theirs/ours. The work is theirs/ours. Just knock for oneself and the door will open.

In contrast to one's Treasure within, this section ends with another jab at material riches, and perhaps even the businesses that are there on the boardwalk.

Don't be like them, consumed by profits, greedy.
Take care of your neighbors who are truly needy.
(Peace out!)

Contemplative Reflection

What does *the Teacher* mean by "recognize what's right in front of you"? How can we cultivate a deeper awareness of the present moment and the truth that lies within our own experience?

This question invites us to reflect on the importance of mindfulness and being present. It challenges us to look

beyond our preconceived notions and to see the truth
that is readily available in the here and now.

What is the significance of *the Teacher's* warning against giving "deep Truths" to those who are not interested or paying attention? How can we discern who is ready to receive such teachings, and how can we share our own insights in a way that is both respectful and effective?

This question encourages us to consider the importance of discernment and skillful communication in sharing spiritual teachings. It prompts us to reflect on how we can offer our own insights in a way that is both meaningful and appropriate for the audience.

Chapter 25 (Sayings 96 - 98)
Awareness in Action

96

"Awareness is like the woman who takes her milk and adds it to the flour to bake large loaves of bread, making it more nutritious and flavorful, as well. Think about what I'm telling you."

97

"Awareness is like a woman who has been carrying a heavy burlap bag of rice down a long path. Its handles have broken, and rice has continuously leaked. When she has come to the end of the road, she's home, where she discovers the bag to be empty."

98

"Awareness is like a man wishing to kill a powerful figure. He takes his knife and stabs it into a wall inside his own house, just to make sure his arm is strong enough and that he has the will to do it. Then he goes and does the deed."

(Standard Translation: Saying 96
Jesus said, "The Father's kingdom can be compared to a woman who took a little yeast and hid it in flour. She made it into large loaves of bread. Anyone who has ears to hear should hear!"

Saying 97
Jesus said, "The Father's kingdom can be compared to a woman carrying a jar of flour. While she was walking down a long road, the jar's handle broke and the flour spilled out behind her on the road. She didn't know it, and didn't realize there was a problem until she got home, put down the jar, and found it empty."

Saying 98
Jesus said, "The Father's kingdom can be compared to a man who wanted to kill someone powerful. He drew his sword in his house and drove it into the wall to figure out

whether his hand was strong enough. Then he killed the powerful one.")

What This Means

I can picture *the Teacher* and the students back at the place they're staying, maybe getting ready for dinner, when the moment comes to teach a little more before their bellies are full and they're winding down. Three quick stories to explain how one understands Awareness and Ultimate Reality.

The first one: It's like a woman, not a man in this case or non-gender specific human, but a woman. And before I get accused of misogyny, it's not because "women belong in the kitchen."

Here is another slight mistranslation of 'leaven,' and it's crucial to the story. It's not likely yeast, since many cases throughout the Bible talk about how it spoils things. That would be flat out evil. The Coptic word for what she adds to the flour is ⲥⲁⲉⲓⲣ or literally "first-milk" or colostrum. It is something that comes from herself for that which is newly birthed, for a beautiful thing.

As any good baker knows, a little milk makes the loaf sweeter, more nourishing, and fluffier. (I had to leave out "anyone who has ears let them hear" at the end, strictly so as not to confuse us with thinking it was "corn" bread. *Wink! Get it? "Ears?"*)

The second: Another woman. In this case, it could be any gender, like the next. In Reality, none of it is gendered.

The woman is carrying a large bag of rice (jar of flour) with a hole (broken handle or "ear"—interesting play on words), causing it to leak. "Oh no! That's terrible!" But is it? That's not what the story says.

It only says she's unaware (maybe not listening to the world around her), and that when she reaches the end of her path, the bag is empty. It's gotten lighter and lighter as she journeyed, and it's not necessarily important that *she didn't realize the problem*. It's just as likely that she didn't see it as problematic. In fact, shedding the weight along the journey is also easing the burden, which is a blessing.

And now, she's Home. Its emptiness speaks to her fullness in the immaterial. There is nothing left to do.

"Bread. Rice. Anyone else getting hungry?"

Just one more story...

Again and again, we see a provocative *Teacher* who likes to turn things upside down and on their head.

This time, Awareness is like a man (although like we said earlier, it could be either. It's just a story.) A man who intends to kill a powerful and popular figure, the type who's getting all the attention. "Whoa! That got dark, quick!" Not to worry—the meaning of this is more like killing one's ego, persona, false self. And that's a figure that does not die easily.

To kill the false self takes some training, perhaps even a good amount of practice. It takes some serious inner strength, and one had better get it right. A wounded ego may hide for a while, but typically comes back when one least expects it, and stronger.

I bet you could hear a pin drop. "Uh, is that the doorbell? We'll go check..."

Contemplative Reflection

How does the metaphor of the woman adding milk to flour to bake bread help us understand the nature of Awareness? What does this suggest about the transformative and nourishing qualities of Consciousness?

This question invites us to reflect on how Awareness from within can enhance and enrich our experience of life. It encourages us to consider how Consciousness can nourish our souls and help us create something meaningful and fulfilling.

What is the significance of the empty bag of rice at the end of the woman's journey? How does this relate to the idea of letting go of attachments and finding liberation in emptiness?

This question prompts us to consider the value of non-attachment and the freedom that comes from releasing our burdens. It suggests that the spiritual journey may involve a process of shedding unnecessary baggage in order to arrive at a place of inner peace and fulfillment.

Chapter 26 (Sayings 99 - 101)
Beyond "By Blood"

99

The students spoke up. "Hey. Your family is right outside waiting for you."

"My family," the Teacher said, "are those who recognize Consciousness. They are with me in Oneness."

100

The group from outside said, "Look at this. The government says we owe them all this money!"

The Teacher said, "You should give the government what belongs to them. Of course, give God what is God's. And give me what's mine, too."

101

"Whoever doesn't completely reject their mom and dad in the way that I do, is not able to learn from me. Sure, my mother gave birth to me, as far as my body goes, but in Reality, it's Consciousness who gave me life."

(Standard Translation: Saying 99
The disciples said to him, "Your brothers and mother are standing outside."
He said to them, "The people here who do the will of my Father are my brothers and mother; they're the ones who will enter my Father's kingdom."

Saying 100
They showed Jesus a gold coin and said to him, "Those who belong to Caesar demand tribute from us."
He said to them, "Give to Caesar what belongs to Caesar, give to God what belongs to God, and give to me what belongs to me."

Saying 101

"Whoever doesn't hate their father and mother as I do can't become my disciple, and whoever doesn't love their father and mother as I do can't become my disciple. For my mother ..., but my true Mother gave me Life.")

What This Means

Saved by the bell. "Oh look! It's your family here to see ya!"

Only in Oneness is anyone "family." Does this seem harsh? Perhaps. Then again, it's been pointed out in John's gospel that we have Jesus calling his mother Mary "woman" since chapter 2, at the wedding at Cana. So, some would say this has been tracking that direction for a while. But that's not necessarily so. We don't have to see it as separating from one's biological family. Remember? *The Teacher* is not really all that big on exclusion. It's more about who is added to our perception of "family" and with regards to this Reality, how folks behave.

"Hey bro! Don't mean to interrupt dinner or anything but look at this—we're getting charged again, fees and fees on top of fees and taxes!"

That's the price we pay for living. Now, what about what you owe God, or what do we owe one another? That is what's worth our attention here.

Mic drop. Door shut.

The Teacher turns back to his students and explains what True Family is. Like I said, there's not necessarily any "hate" for the people in one's biological family, but there must be a rejection of both the limitation and label it has. One's "siblings" are those who also recognize their connection to Source. Each and every one is *its* manifestation, *its* children. *Consciousness gave us life*, before we were even born.

Now go wash up...

Contemplative Reflection

What does *the Teacher* mean by saying that their true family are those who "recognize Consciousness"? How does this challenge our conventional understanding of family and belonging?

This question prompts us to consider the deeper meaning of family and community. It invites us to reflect on the possibility that our spiritual connections can be just as strong, if not stronger, than our biological ties.

How does *the Teacher's* response to the question about taxes and obligations to the government relate to their overall message about spiritual priorities? What does this suggest about the balance between fulfilling our worldly duties and pursuing our spiritual path?

This question encourages us to consider the relationship between our spiritual lives and our responsibilities in the world. It challenges us to find a way to navigate these seemingly competing demands in a way that is both ethical and fulfilling.

Chapter 27 (Sayings 102 - 106)
Beyond Dogma

102

"Dogmatists are completely contemptible. They act like territorial pets sleeping on the hay in a cattle barn. It neither eats the hay itself nor lets the cows eat any either."

103

"It's important to know where a thief will try to break in. One can then gather up everything they need and be ready for it."

104

The students said, "Oh, we need to be prepared? Let's do this. Let's get down and pray and fast, right here, right now."

"Hold on. Have I done something wrong that I need to confess and make right?" the Teacher asked.

"Wait until one walks away from Oneness. Then you can pray and fast all you want."

105

"Sadly, one who knows Source and Consciousness as their True Parent will be left out and bullied as an illegitimate offspring of a whore."

106

"Whenever you make two into One, then you— the child of Consciousness—can face anything, no matter how big it seems."

(Standard Translation: Saying 102
Jesus said, "How awful for the Pharisees who are like a dog sleeping in a feeding trough for cattle, because the dog doesn't eat, and doesn't let the cattle eat either."

Saying 103
Jesus said, "Blessed is the one who knows where the bandits are going to enter. They can] get up to assemble their defenses and be

prepared to defend themselves before they arrive."

Saying 104

They said to Jesus, "Come, let's pray and fast today."

Jesus said, "What have I done wrong? Have I failed?

"Rather, when the groom leaves the bridal chamber, then people should fast and pray."

Saying 105

Jesus said, "Whoever knows their father and mother will be called a bastard."

Saying 106

Jesus said, "When you make the two into one, you'll become Children of Humanity, and if you say 'Mountain, go away!', it'll go.")

What This Means

The Teacher is on a rant. Understandably so. We all know that an unannounced visit by the so-called "fam" who showed up just to whine would surely sour anyone's grapes. They could have been sitting down and trying to eat, when suddenly all this nonsense just kept gnawing away at *the Teacher*.

What is it with people who push doctrine and "dog"ma? (See what I did there?) They act like they're so much better than anyone. To make it worse, they see their own spirituality as selective and superior to others, and then they exclude everyone who doesn't look and sound just like them. But, in Real life, they know nothing about it! *Grrrr...*

It starts to calm down. Perhaps *the Teacher* is noticing the students all staring with eyes wide and mouths agape. *The Teacher* tells them how wonderful it is to be able to recognize these hypocrites, and how important it is to be on the lookout.

"Yeah totally. Here, let's all grab hands and pray in agreement. Come on, confession is good for the soul."

Facepalm, again. *Pray in agreement? And what would I need to confess? What sin do you think I'm struggling with here?*

Tell ya what, wait until someone rejects Reality. You can pray and fast all you want with them. Meanwhile, pass the potatoes...

I would think that *the Teacher* at this point may have taken a few bites before circling back to their point.

The truth is, when one starts *vib'ing* with Consciousness—when they see that everything and everyone belongs, treating it all as equal and not just for the select few in the right group—there's going to be some serious backlash and scorn.

Take a deep breath. Relax. And remember, recognizing Oneness is a thing which transmutes obstacles, and what moves mountains. That was also back in Saying 48.

Contemplative Reflection

How does *the Teacher's* critique of dogmatists relate to their overall message about the importance of direct spiritual experience and the limitations of rigid belief systems?

This question encourages us to reflect on the dangers and distractions of dogmatism and the importance of keeping an open mind on the spiritual path. It prompts us to consider how rigid beliefs can hinder our understanding and prevent us from experiencing the deeper truth.

What does *the Teacher* mean by advising us to "know where a thief will try to break in"? How can we cultivate awareness of our own vulnerabilities and prepare ourselves for potential challenges on the spiritual path?

This question invites us to examine our own weaknesses and blind spots. It encourages us to develop a proactive approach to spiritual practice, anticipating potential obstacles and cultivating the inner resources to navigate them with wisdom and resilience.

Chapter 28 (Sayings 107 - 112)
Beyond Boundaries

107

"Consciousness is also like a rancher who had a hundred livestock animals. When the largest of them wandered off, the rancher searched and searched until it was found. Completely exhausted, the rancher said, 'I absolutely love you—you're my favorite one!' "

108

As Oneness, the Teacher said, "Intoxicate yourself from what flows from my mouth, and you will become me. I will become you, too, and anything that's unknown will become completely clear."

109

"True Awareness is like a person who owned a field with buried treasure and died not even knowing about it. The child who inherited the field also didn't know anything was there and sold it.

"The buyer decided to plow it, discovered the treasure and began to loan money with interest to anyone who came along."

110

"Anyone who has learned Real Value and has had a good look at how material value is measured, can forget about the scales."

111

"For those scouring through stacks of books trying to explain how everything is just a matter of form and function, objects and concepts, science and philosophies, try to understand instead how Consciousness can't be found in something that has a 'The End.' Find your True Self and you'll realize how cheap physical things and mental concepts actually are."

112

"It's terrible for the one whose flesh clings to a Soul! And just as bad for the Soul who clings to a body!"

(Standard Translation: Saying 107
Jesus said, "The kingdom can be compared to a shepherd who had a hundred sheep. The largest one strayed. He left the ninety-nine and looked for that one until he found it. Having gone through the trouble, he said to the sheep: 'I love you more than the ninety-nine.' "

Saying 108
Jesus said, "Whoever drinks from my mouth will become like me, and I myself will become like them; then, what's hidden will be revealed to them."

Saying 109
Jesus said, "The kingdom can be compared to someone who had a treasure hidden in their field. They didn't know about it. After they died, they left it to their son. The son

didn't know it either. He took the field and sold it.

"The buyer plowed the field, found the treasure, and began to loan money at interest to whomever they wanted."

Saying 110
Jesus said, "Whoever has found the world and become rich should renounce the world."

Saying 111
Jesus said, "The heavens and the earth will roll up in front of you, and whoever lives from the Living One won't see death."
Doesn't Jesus say, "Whoever finds themselves, of them the world isn't worthy"?

Saying 112
Jesus said, "How awful for the flesh that depends on the soul. How awful for the soul that depends on the flesh.")

What This Means

There's no hint to whether this is at the same meal, if they're hanging out during a different meal, or if they're eating at all. We do know that meeting and eating together was a pretty common practice in antiquity, especially among early groups like this. So we'll play like it is.

Both the original and standard translations have the next story about sheep—which most of us don't regularly encounter. It could have been a herd of cattle or goats, instead, or backyard chickens, for that matter. It wouldn't make any difference.

Saying 107 is related to the parable of the lost sheep spoken about in Luke 15 and Matthew 18. Both synoptic parallels say of the sheep that it's one who wanders off from the flock, and the shepherd leaves the 99 to rescue it. Although, in Luke 15, the Heavenly Father rescues the "repentant lost sheep and angels all rejoice."

Matthew 18 adds how "God's unwilling that any of the precious little ones should perish."

The perspective in the Gospel of Thomas is different. First, it's not just a sheep, but the *biggest* sheep—like a huge fish or a great big pearl. Also, the Coptic here is beautiful: ⲁ ⲟⲩⲁ ⲛ̄ ⲑⲏⲧ ⲟⲩ ⲥⲱⲣⲙ` It translates to *did one of heart and mind go astray.* In essence, the sheep went in a different direction from the rest. As one probably should, right? The parable ends with the shepherd finding and telling the rescued sheep that it is the most-loved one, *desired above the rest combined.*

The next Saying (108) also has a similar gospel parallel in John 17, "I have given them the glory that you gave me, that they may be one as we are one—I in them and you in me—so that they may be brought to complete unity."

The Teacher is all about the recognition of Oneness. One with them, with Source or Father, with each other, with the entire universe, seen and unseen. One great, big Oneness. That's the Ultimate Reality.

Then we get an interesting story: how Consciousness is like a person who unknowingly has a hidden treasure within. "Whoa! Like a pearl?" That's doubtful. Consciousness would know about something like that.

It's something else. And for the offspring—who are "heirs" who also recognize Reality—it doesn't register as anything of Real Value either. We may remember that Saying 45 shows there's good treasure and evil treasure (where good people have what's stored inside them and others, well, what's stored in them). What we see next in the story is someone who takes whatever it is from them and makes enough profit to start loan sharking. Uh oh...

So, what is the treasure? It must be something Oneness doesn't value. Of course it could be something that seems spiritual. One doesn't have to look hard to see that the business of gurus, self-improvement and religious personalities are all billion-dollar businesses. Spirituality is easily synthesized. It's a drug with millions of addicts.

Honestly, you and I can spend a fortune filling bookshelves with books that claim to have all the answers. Now, I'm not suggesting that we ban or burn books, or say they're not helpful, and neither does *the Teacher*. But the proof is in eating the pudding, not collecting pudding recipes. Right? That's even more true of Consciousness, which has no "start here, do this, and now you're done." In pudding-talk, Consciousness is a delicious, big, bottomless bowl.

Contemplative Reflection

What is the significance of the parable about the rancher and the lost livestock? How does this story illustrate the idea that perhaps there are paths worth "wandering forth" from, and how we are always loved and supported by Consciousness?

This question invites us to consider courage and discernment, as well as the unconditionality and undergirding of Consciousness. It prompts us to reflect on how this boundless love extends to all beings, even when one may appear or feel lost or disconnected.

What does *the Teacher* mean by the invitation to "intoxicate yourself from what flows from my mouth"? How can we open ourselves to the teachings and insights that can lead us to a deeper experience of Oneness?

This question encourages us to consider the transformative power of the Teacher's words and teachings. It challenges us to actively engage with these teachings and allow them to nourish and inspire our spiritual journey.

How does the parable of the hidden treasure in the field relate to the concept of discernment? What does this story teach us even about spiritual charlatans?

This question prompts us to reflect on evaluating what's of Real Value and what's not for each of us. It suggests that, like the treasure in the field, we should be aware of what we're buying into.

Chapter 29 (Sayings 113 & 114)
Beyond Bias

113

The students asked, "When does Enlightenment happen?"

"It's not something you can just watch for and wait on," said the Teacher, "No one can point it out for you by saying, 'There it is!' or 'Oh, that's it!' The Presence of Oneness is always everywhere, even though no one seems to perceive it."

114

The one called the Boulder said, "We should dismiss the female student, since this isn't something for women."

The Teacher replied, "How about this: I'll guide her myself as she continues to show her intelligence, courage, self-control, and honor.

That way she will embody Oneness and be an equal.

"Because anyone who recognizes their True Self is wholly transformed by and as Consciousness."

(Standard Translation: Saying 113
His disciples said to him, "When will the kingdom come?"
"It won't come by looking for it. They won't say, 'Look over here!' or 'Look over there!' Rather, the Father's kingdom is already spread out over the earth, and people don't see it."

Saying 114
Simon Peter said to them, "Mary should leave us, because women aren't worthy of life."
Jesus said, "Look, am I to make her a man? So that she may become a living spirit too, she's equal to you men, because every woman who makes herself manly will enter the kingdom of heaven.")

What This Means

The students are still looking for proof, a sign, anything to have Reality all spelled out for them. *It just doesn't work that way, folks. If ya still can't tell that it's right here and all around us, you've already missed it.*

It's interesting that most of the writings outside of the Bible show disagreements between the disciples and a number of diverse communities' understanding of Jesus.

It is evident even within the Bible, such as the Gospel of Luke and Acts of the Apostles stories, that they try to clean it up with extra post-crucifixion and additional "miracle" accounts. The truth is that by the third and fourth centuries, a strategic "unified" belief system was at the top of the political and social agenda of the day. Christianity rapidly went from the sentencing of marginalization and martyrdom to holding the winning ticket for popularity and power.

Leave it to Peter in the original and translated texts. *"I bet it's because Mary is holding us back. You should dismiss her. That way, we won't keep being slowed down and can finally be taken seriously."*

The very end of the Gospel of Thomas makes a huge statement. We know that throughout Judaic and Christian history, patriarchy has always raised its ugly head, and it was no less the attitude of Rome than it was at the Temple in antiquity. Of course, it's behavior that defined the masculine more than biology at this time. Yet Jesus was incredibly subversive, insisting on equality. Exactly how could Oneness possibly be anything else? And even though we do not read of her saying anything here, Mary was *the Tower*.

And this is how *the Teacher* ends it: Recognize your True Self. See that it is all embracing, all imbuing, completely colorful, gender-ful, beautiful, non-dual Consciousness.

What a great bookend from where we started, with *the Teacher* telling us that "there's no stopping the deeply searching person," and then this gospel ends here with "You are the One you must find."

Contemplative Reflection

How can we shift our focus from seeking Enlightenment as a future event to recognizing the Presence of Oneness in the here and now? What practices or perspectives might help us perceive this ever-present reality?

This question challenges us to reframe our understanding of Enlightenment as a state of being that is always available, rather than a distant goal. It encourages us to cultivate a greater awareness of the present moment and to recognize the Divine presence in our everyday experiences.

How does *the Teacher's* defense of *the Tower* (Mary Magdalene) challenge the patriarchal attitudes and assumptions that were prevalent in their time and continue to exist today? What can we learn from this about the importance of recognizing the equality and inherent worth of all beings?

This question invites us to reflect on the Teacher's radical stance on equality and inclusion. It encourages us to examine our own biases and to work towards creating a more just and equitable world where all voices are valued and respected.

This is where Thomas ends, and Mary begins...

I mean sure, you can go grab a beverage, some popcorn, use the restroom if you want, but the Gospel of Thomas ends here. While there's no early text that suggests that the Gospel of Mary was written to follow that of Thomas, there are striking similarities that allow them to fit nicely together.

For one, the Gospel of Thomas doesn't really have an end story. There's no narrative around Jesus' arrest or death (or resurrection) like we have in other canonical gospels. Aside from its similarity of teachings, what we have of the Gospel of Mary drops us in the middle of the story, towards the end of Jesus' life—at least the end of his time with his disciples.

It's missing its first 6 of 19 pages (as well as pages 11 - 14). There's speculation that the beginning of the Gospel of Mary may follow a death and resurrection narrative. After all, Mary Magdalene appears in each of the canonical gospel's post-Easter stories, but we really don't even have a hint.

Page seven begins right in the middle of a scene before "the Savior" leaves. (We are making the assumption it's Jesus, since it's the same basic scenario we have in the Bible and similar texts, but it doesn't explicitly name "the Savior.")

What we find in these fragments that remain of Mary's Gospel is that they seem to at least fit with Thomas' Gospel (and John's too) rather nicely. Let's take a look at it.

Note: Because the Gospel of Mary is missing its front and middle pages before ending on page 19, there's not really a widely accepted numbering other than the page numbers that the early copies we have denote. So that's what you see here, too.

MAGGIE'S GOSPEL

(Pages 1 - 6 are missing)

Chapter 30 (Page 7a)
Consciousness and Creation

The students asked, "Can you explain something about the material world? Does it last forever?"

"Everything that is manifest as physical—that is, what is natural, elemental, 'made' so to say of matter—exists in a way that is entangled with everything else," the Teacher replied. "It's all connected in Reality, and its materiality will be dissolved back into Consciousness eventually. Do you remember when I taught you that 'everything comes from Source and everything returns to it?' It's important that you try to understand this."

(Standard Translation:
"Then will [matter] be [destroyed], or not?"
The Savior said, "Every nature, every form, every creature exists in and with each other,

but they'll dissolve again into their own roots, because the nature of matter dissolves into its nature alone. Anyone who has ears to hear should hear!")

What This Means

It's too bad there's no copies of the first six pages (yet! Fingers crossed we discover those!), but the fragments we do have are pretty sweet.

We just touched a little on the material world towards the end of the Gospel of Thomas. What we start with here feels like it could easily click right in with those. Perhaps it's a different perspective from the same conversation, or maybe another case of *the Teacher* (Jesus) coming back to it. Either way, it explains the relationship between the material world and Consciousness quite nicely.

It also brings in concepts like we find in the Upanishad, as well as in quantum physics, where matter is supposed as a condensing and

solidifying of Spirit. In Hindu philosophy,
Prakriti (प्रकृति) refers to the primal matter that
gives rise to the material world. It's that all–
pervading, underlying, eternal essence that
constitutes the universe. Saying 77 of Thomas'
Gospel also hints at Spirit underlying all
material reality, "Chop and split a chunk of
wood, and you will see that I have embodied it.
Look to see what's hiding under a rock, and I
am there, too."

Both gospels (here and in Sayings 49 & 77)
address how everything originates from and
dissolves back into Source. Some folks are
bound to relate all of this with esoteric concepts
of "energy," or compare it to the vibratory
pulsation of consciousness similar to *Spanda*
(स्पन्द) in Tantric Shaivism. I don't think we *have*
to take deep dives into a vast array of
metaphysical systems to see that there's a basic
understanding which they all share. To me, this
is very interesting. Each of these different

perceptions of Light reflect and refract on their own facet, but together they glimmer, glisten, shimmer and sparkle. And I can't look away.

Contemplative Reflection

How does the concept of matter "dissolving back into Consciousness" challenge our everyday understanding of the physical world? How might this perspective shift our relationship to material possessions and our sense of self?

This question encourages us to reconsider the nature of reality and the impermanence of material forms. It prompts us to reflect on how our attachment to material possessions might be hindering our spiritual growth.

In what ways can we deepen our understanding of the interconnectedness of all things, as emphasized by *the Teacher's* statement that "everything is connected in Reality"? How might this understanding foster a greater sense of compassion and responsibility towards all beings?

This question invites us to explore the implications of the interconnectedness of all things. It encourages us to consider how this understanding can inform our actions and relationships, fostering a greater sense of empathy and responsibility towards all of creation.

Chapter 31 (Pages 7b - 8a)
What's Iniquity, What's Harmony

The one they called the Boulder asked, "Since you're already explaining all this, can I add a question? What does it mean when people talk about 'the sin of the world?' Is it the material world that's bad or what?"

The Teacher said, "First, you must realize that sin is just a concept, not a Real thing. When one chooses to behave like materiality is reality, separated from the Divine, and engages with this belief, that is how sin is manifested. And this is why Awareness reveals itself as the True Self, which in turn draws and reconstitutes the essence of everything back into Source."

"But, if one is tricked into giving their attention to mere materiality, setting their affection on things, they become sick and lifeless. If you get what I'm saying, hold on to it."

"It's the attachments one has with things in this material world that causes suffering. Why? Because everything that is perceived as being only physical goes against the True Nature of Reality. It throws one's body out of balance and disturbs their Natural harmony. But wholeness is restored when one finds contentment as it manifests in all forms—no matter how seemingly different. This is the True Self and Awareness of Presence. So, hear me out."

(Standard Translation:
Peter said to him, "Since you've explained everything to us, tell us one more thing. What's the sin of the world?"

The Savior said, "Sin doesn't exist, but you're the ones who make sin when you act in accordance with the nature of adultery, which is called 'sin.' That's why the Good came among you, up to the things of every nature in order to restore it within its root."

Then he continued and said, "That's why you get sick and die, because [you love what tricks you. Anyone who] can understand should understand!

"Matter [gave birth to] a passion that has no image because it comes from what's contrary to nature. Then confusion arises in the whole body. That's why I told you to be content at heart. If you're discontented, find contentment in the presence of the various images of nature. Anyone who has ears to hear should hear!")

What This Means

Silly, stubborn *Boulder* (Peter). "Yeah, thanks for explaining everything, but you left out the part about how the world sins because they're born that way, and they go to be punished and tortured for it forever and ever in a fiery hell. And how since we asked you into our hearts, we're better and we go to heaven, right?"

No doubt, *the Teacher* will be bringing over the facepalms from Thomas' Gospel here. *My brother in Jesus (wink!), there's no such thing as original sin.*

What we call "sin" is what we distort and deny, not what we inherited in our DNA from Adam and Eve's fall. Then *the Teacher* seems to review much of what was covered earlier—recapping materiality, how we're united with the Divine, the recognition of Awareness, being distracted by trivial things, attachments and suffering, the wholeness of our True Self.

This, too, is echoed across so–called religious lines. In Buddhist doctrine, there is a key concept called *upādāna* (उपादान) that refers to clinging, grasping, and attachment. It is thought to be the by-product of *taṇhā*, or craving, which is part of the *dukkha*, or suffering.

Looking again in the Bhagavad Gita (5.10), we find this:

ब्रह्मण्याधाय कर्माणि सङ्गं त्यक्त्वा करोति यः ।

लिप्यते न स पापेन पद्मपत्रमिवाम्भसा ॥

brahmaṇyādhāya karmāṇi
saṅgaṁ tyaktvā karoti yaḥ
lipyate na sa pāpena padma-patram
ivāmbhasā

Meaning this: Those who dedicate their actions to God, abandoning all attachment, remain untouched by sin, just as a lotus leaf is untouched by water.

Wu Wei in Taoism is the means by which we let go of our expectations and attachments to outcomes.

I think it's also somewhat helpful to realize that among the earliest waves of Christianity was an identity focused on the Good, or *Chrestos*. Standard translations here read, "This is why 'the Good' (emphasis mine) has come into your midst." Christianity which focuses on the worship of the Messiah/Anointed (*Christos*) was likely developed somewhat separately and even capitalized on later.

We also find more about Nature and Reality, and how it's rooted to Source, and how it's just *killing* us being trapped in our own sensory and mental perspectives! Of course, by Nature, we're not really talking about Mother Nature, not birds and bees, flowers and trees, a refreshing breeze—although all these are nice and are included in the concept; it's just more than that.

Nature in the Gospel of Mary has to do with the Presence of the Divine in its form *and* beyond it, echoing Thomas' Gospel, as Saying 83 states:

"Images manifest, appearing from within people, but the Light that's inside of them is hidden by the Light of Awareness. It will be revealed, but beyond figure and form it stays obscured by its Light."

It's not just the "likeness" we're created in, but the "image" as well. We are spiritual and physical beings. Surely this is what *the Teacher* means at the beginning of the text, how "Ultimate Reality is right here, *both* within you and everywhere around you." This is why one finds nature so peaceful—by discovering that the Divine Image penetrates and manifests in and as nature.

Contemplative Reflection

How does the concept of "sin" as a manifestation of separation from the Divine challenge traditional religious views of sin as an inherent moral failing?

This question prompts us to consider sin not as a fixed state, but as a consequence of our choices and beliefs. It encourages a shift in perspective from guilt and shame towards understanding and reconnection.

How can we cultivate contentment and balance in a world that often encourages attachment and dissatisfaction? What practices or perspectives can help us align with our True Nature and find harmony within ourselves and the world around us?

This question invites us to explore practical ways to overcome the pull of material desires and find inner peace. It encourages us to seek practices that promote mindfulness, gratitude, and a deeper connection to our True Self.

In what ways does the Teacher's message about the interconnectedness of all things resonate with contemporary ecological and social justice movements? How can this understanding inspire action towards healing our relationship with the planet and each other?

This question bridges the ancient wisdom of the text with current global challenges. It prompts us to consider how the Teacher's message of interconnectedness can inform our approach to environmental sustainability and social responsibility.

Chapter 32 (Pages 8b - 9a)
Farewell and Share Well

The Teacher then gave each of the students a final embrace. "It's time for me to leave your company, but I am always with you and you with me. So, attend to one another patiently and peacefully, as I have with you."

"Remember what I taught you. Be wary of those who try to say, 'You have to go this way' or 'it's up or out there.' Remember that you are the Living Manifestation of the Living Source. We are truly Human and Divine. Remember that what you have searched deeply for will be revealed. Go and get out there and share this! So many are still searching!"

"But when you do this, don't add anything to what you've been taught. When you make up all these extra rules, it traps you like religious dogma does, and it's not about doctrine. Okay?" Shortly after this, the Teacher left.

(Standard Translation:

When the Blessed One said these things, he greeted them all and said, "Peace be with you! Acquire my peace. Be careful not to let anyone mislead you by saying, 'Look over here!' or 'Look over there!' Because the Son of Humanity exists within you. Follow him! Those who seek him will find him.

"Go then and preach the gospel about the kingdom. Don't lay down any rules beyond what I've given you, nor make a law like the lawgiver, lest you be bound by it." When he said these things, he left.)

What This Means

It's wild how many times we read about Jesus warning folks concerning those who will try to tell you that God's up there in heaven or out there somewhere—all places outside of ourselves. And they're wrong! We saw it back in Sayings 3, 10, and 82, and right here as well, with one foot out the door as one of the last things he says.

For reasons not explained in the text, *the Teacher* must leave. I have no desire to merge the other post–Easter stories here that seem to have been added to the overall Jesus narrative. These are not only unnecessary to his message, but distracting. *Don't go adding to what I've taught you!* And just like Israel does when Moses takes leave to have a quick chat with God on Mount Sinai—making a baby cow idol out of gold—we will see Jesus' disciples in a like manner. *Oh, and please don't make this harder than it is. I've explained all this again and again. Go out and share just these things I've shared with you. I gotta go. Peace out.*

Contemplative Reflection

How does *the Teacher's* emphasis on avoiding additional rules and dogma challenge traditional religious practices? In what ways might this approach foster a more direct and personal spiritual experience?

This question encourages us to consider the potential limitations of rigid religious structures and to explore the benefits of a more flexible and individualized approach to spirituality.

What is the significance of *the Teacher's* final message to "go and share" the teachings? How can we actively embody this call to action in our own lives and communities, while remaining true to *the Teacher's* warning against adding unnecessary dogma?

This question prompts us to consider our responsibility to spread the Teacher's message of love, unity, and self-discovery. It challenges us to find ways to share these teachings authentically and effectively, without imposing our own interpretations or beliefs onto others.

Chapter 33 (Page 9b)

Grieving and Believing

The students were flooded with emotions— sadness, anger, confusion. "We're 'what' again? 'The Living Manifestation from the Living Source,' From 'something-or-another' of the 'live source,' and what else? How are we supposed to share all this? And who again did he want us to tell it to? And if there were people who didn't like hearing what he said, they're going to hate us, probably even try to hurt us! How is this even a good thing at all!"

Although the Tower was grieving deeply too, she stood up, hugging and comforting the other students. "I know how hard this is, but we can't get stuck in this sorrow. We can't start having all these doubts. The Teacher has given us such grace and remains united with us in our hearts. The Teacher will continue to guide, to comfort, to teach us from this place. We can be thankful that we have each other and are honestly prepared to do this work. This is what becoming fully Human and recognizing our True Self is all about, right?"

After saying this, the other students turned their attention inward as the Tower reminded them and began to sort out what the Teacher meant by all the things shared with them.

(Standard Translation:
But they grieved and wept bitterly. They said, "How can we go up to the Gentiles to preach the gospel about the kingdom of the Son of Humanity? If they didn't spare him, why would they spare us?"

Then Mary arose and greeted them all. She said to her brothers (and sisters), "Don't weep and grieve or let your hearts be divided, because his grace will be with you all and will protect you. Rather we should praise his greatness because he's prepared us and made us Humans."

When Mary said these things, she turned their hearts [toward] the Good and they [started] to debate the words of [the Savior].)

What This Means

Well, maybe the Teacher's peace will come in due time. Right now, we're all pretty freaked out. And sad. And mad. And confused. All legitimate feelings one should feel, really. But let's not get crazy.

Mary—who undoubtedly felt the full spectrum of feelings, especially given her relationship to Jesus obviously being the closest!)—seems to move quickly with empathy and compassion. While the rest were panicking over what would happen to themselves, she immediately moves in to comfort those around her. I can hardly imagine a more fully Human/Divine attribute. She gets it, and either sets aside her need to process her emotions or perhaps integrates them into Oneness. Her Love tugs on the other students' hearts, at least at first. They seem to be trying to bring their attention back to all that *the Teacher* shared with them... right before arguing again...

Contemplative Reflection

How does *the Tower's* response to the students' grief and confusion demonstrate leadership and resilience? What can we learn from her example about navigating challenging emotions and staying focused on our spiritual purpose?

This question encourages reflection on the Tower's ability to provide comfort and guidance in a time of crisis. It prompts us to consider how we can cultivate similar qualities of leadership and resilience in our own lives.

In what ways does *the Teacher's* absence create an opportunity for the students to deepen their understanding and embodiment of the teachings? How can we actively engage with spiritual teachings even when our teachers or guides are no longer physically present?

This question invites us to explore the potential for growth and transformation that can arise from periods of uncertainty and change. It challenges us to take ownership of our own spiritual development and to find ways to connect with the teachings on a deeper level.

Chapter 34 (Page 10a)
Perception and Presence

Then the Boulder asked the Tower, "Everyone knows the Teacher had a thing for you. Can you tell us everything that you learned straight from him? I'm sure there were lots of things the Teacher explained better to you than us."

"I can try. Like the Teacher told us all along, 'what seems hidden from our perception will then be revealed.'"

"As far as anything else I can share that might help, I can tell you about a Dream I had, where I felt the Teacher's Presence instructing me. It's funny. I remember it began with me even saying, *'Teacher, I can see you right here in my dream.'*"

(Standard Translation:

Peter said to Mary, "Sister, we know the Savior loved you more than all other women. Tell us the words of the Savior that you remember – the things which you know that we don't, and which we haven't heard."

In response Mary said, "I'll tell you what's hidden from you." So she started to tell them these words: "I," she said, "I saw the Lord in a vision and I said to him, 'Lord, I saw you in a vision today.')

What This Means

This guy really is dense, isn't he? Forget about how she is putting everyone else ahead of herself. Although he acknowledges she must be the most hurt by *the Teacher's* leaving, he's more worried about his personal FOMO (fear of missing out).

Still moved by her empathy and by Love, she shares her innermost insight from her deepest

Dream. This was her experience with the Divine, and she offers it to others, a mirror of what *the Teacher* would do. She positions the Light to illuminate the Path she had walked with *the Teacher* so they could see.

Contemplative Reflection

What is the significance of *the Tower* sharing her dream experience with the other disciples? How does this act reflect *the Teacher's* teachings about sharing knowledge and illuminating the path for others?

This question encourages reflection on the importance of sharing personal spiritual experiences for the benefit of the community. It prompts us to consider how our own insights and revelations can serve to guide and inspire others on their spiritual journeys.

How does *the Tower's* dream experience, where she sees and interacts with *the Teacher*, offer a potential model for maintaining a connection with spiritual guidance even after a teacher's physical absence?

This question invites contemplation on the possibility of continued spiritual connection and guidance through dreams, memories, or intuition. It prompts us to explore ways to cultivate our own inner wisdom and maintain a sense of connection to Oneness.

Chapter 35 (Page 10b)
The Meeting Place

"You're so lucky this doesn't freak you out," the Teacher said. "It's wonderful you can realize that the Awareness rises up here in the heartmind, where Humanity and Divinity intertwine."

"How is it," I asked, "that all this happens? How can I see here? Is it with my soul? My spirit?"

"It's not either really. At least not on their own. It's what rises up in-between, like the Stillpoint..."

The Tower continued to share all the things from the Dream and how she understood it.

(Standard Translation:
"In response he said to me, 'You're blessed because you didn't waver at the sight of me. For where the mind is, there is the treasure.'

"I said to him, 'Lord, now does the one who sees the vision see it in the soul or in the spirit?'

"In response the Savior said, 'They don't see in the soul or in the spirit, but the mind which exists between the two is what sees the vision and it that ...)

What This Means

I love how it begins with a *Wow! It's so cool; you're not freaking out.* What we read in the original text here is the concept of unwavering, and it's interesting to see it contrasts with how the other students are reacting.

It's also helpful to understand that in its context there is a concept of the Immovable Race, or Unshakable Generation, as Shirley Paulson points out in her book *Illuminating the Secret Revelation of John* (another fascinating extra-canonical text!)

"This 'generation' or 'race' (neither word a perfect translation) consisted of those who either were willing or ready to hear the spiritual ideas... Controlling passions (thoughts) was the key to living in the realm of God's order, the original state of harmony and stillness."

We'll see this unfold even more as we continue.

Then, there's the acknowledgement of "where the *nous is*, there lies the treasure," a popular phrase quoted throughout the first century by the likes of Clement, Justin and Macarios. It reminds me of Eckhart, too, when he writes of perceiving from the heartmind, "The Eye with which I see God is the eye that he sees me."

It's interesting how we find in ancient times various practices of contemplation by way of "having a bird's eye view." The term *metanoia* (μετάνοια) lends itself to "change one's mind" in a way that implies transcending it or bringing awareness to itself. In Jungian psychology, as well, there is an insight to be received from such "visions from above." Visions were not hallucinations, nor were they mere dreams, but big "D" Dreams like direct encounters with the Divine we read throughout scriptures and inspired texts.

Here inside *the Tower's* Dream, we find *the Teacher* answering her question about how she is able to perceive any of this. It's explained as coming from the heartmind, which is that shared space-within connected to both the Human and Divine.

If you remember from early in the first part, *the Teacher* tells a story of how Awareness of the True Self is like a girl who "loves to fish, putting her whole head and heart into it." The sea could be seen as the part of Consciousness belonging to both the Kingdom-within and where it penetrates the "outside" world, too. She has "caught" who she is in Reality, recognizing her True Self. She *is* the Big Fish that's worth casting all the little fish back into the sea.

Contemplative Reflection

What is the significance of the "heartmind" as the place where "Humanity and Divinity intertwine"? How can we cultivate a greater awareness of this sacred space within ourselves?

This question invites exploration of the heartmind as a bridge between our human experience and our divine nature. It encourages practices that foster a deeper connection to this inner space, such as meditation, contemplation, and self-reflection.

What is the meaning of the "Stillpoint" that arises "in-between" the soul and spirit? How can we cultivate a greater awareness of this

Stillpoint and its role in our spiritual development?

This question invites contemplation on the Stillpoint as a place of balance and integration within ourselves. It encourages us to explore practices that can help us access this state of stillness and deepen our connection to our True Self.

(Pages 11 – 14 are missing)

The next few pages are ones we do not have and cannot see. Perhaps what is missing is to be filled in for us as seen by the Eye of our own Heart, too. In a way, what we are left with in the empty space is an invitation to Dream for ourselves.

Take a Moment to Gaze

Imagine what your "Eye of the Heart" could have witnessed in these five missing pages...

Chapter 36 (Page 15a)
True Self's Identity

"...Then a figure called The Craving stood and spoke up, "Although I didn't really notice you sneaking in, here you are trying to make a stand, thinking that you've tricked me. Don't you know? You're under my spell! I control you!"

"Afraid not," said the True Self, "You've never seen me and know nothing about me, but I know you. All you've done is tricked yourself, mistaking my clothing for me."

Having said this, the True Self walked right on by, with a pocketful of joy and a soft smile.

(Standard Translation:
"And Desire said, 'I didn't see you going down, but now I see you're going up. So why are you lying, since you belong to me?'

"In response the soul said, 'I saw you, but you didn't see me or know me. I was to you just a garment, and you didn't recognize me.' When it said these things, it left, rejoicing greatly.)

What This Means

The Dream seems to pick back up where *the Tower* has started into a "second level." Was there a set up and first level in the missing pages? We can only assume.

The journey is reminiscent of an ascension of the soul, not unlike what we find later in The Cloud of Unknowing or even Teresa of Avila's Interior Castle.

We have nothing here about the level before—which we can assume was The Obscuring (Darkness), as seen in the list to come (and from another text mentioned later; we'll get to that soon enough)—but on this one, *the Tower* is confronted by Craving (Desire).

Personally, when I read how Desire or Craving addressed her, I was instantly drawn back to the memory of my own encounter with Addiction. It wielded "craving" like a weapon which left a lasting sting upon each blow. It was not until I began to recognize my True Self that I found freedom from the objects of addiction and the truth about what lies behind these objects—the lie of who I thought, what I was told, I was. This identity which held itself in separation from the Divine, differed from my True Self. The Real "I" was unscathed, though my "clothes" showed the slash.

Contemplative Reflection

How does the interaction between the True Self and Craving (Desire) reflect the struggle between our authentic nature and our conditioned desires? How can we recognize and overcome the ways in which our cravings may obscure our True Self?

This question encourages us to explore the internal conflict between our deeper being and the surface-level desires that can lead us astray. It prompts us to consider how mindfulness and self-awareness can help us distinguish between Oneness and the fleeting cravings that can keep us from experiencing our authentic selves.

What is the significance of the True Self's ability to see through Craving's deception and recognize its true nature? How can we cultivate this level of discernment in our own lives to navigate the challenges and temptations that may arise on the spiritual path?

This question emphasizes the importance of developing inner wisdom and discernment to see through the illusions and distractions that can hinder our spiritual progress. It invites us to consider practices such as meditation, self-reflection, and seeking guidance from trusted mentors to cultivate a deeper understanding of ourselves and the world around us.

Chapter 37 (Page 15b)
True Self and Source

The True Self approached the third level. There stood a large figure they called The Ignorance, who drew in closely, probing them.

"Exactly where do you think you're going?" Ignorance laughed and scowled. "You have no rights, no permission. You're nothing but a prisoner to your addictions, without even a clue what to do, let alone what's right or wrong. You're worthless!"

"You—like many—have done nothing but criticize me, though I don't judge anyone," said the True Self, "I've been dominated, but haven't even pushed for my own agency. Although I'm not given any acknowledgment, I completely recognize this: everything comes from Source and returns to Source. Heaven and Earth, as they say,

will pass away; it's impermanent and will be released in every form."

(Standard Translation:

"Again, it came to the third power, which is called 'Ignorance.' [It] interrogated the soul and [said], 'Where are you going? In wickedness you're bound. Since you're bound, don't judge!'

"[And] the soul said, 'Why do you judge me, since I haven't judged? I was bound, even though I haven't bound. They didn't recognize me, but I've recognized that everything will dissolve – both the things of the [earth] and the things of [heaven].')

What This Means

From here, the proverbial escalator takes us to Ignorance. But this is no ordinary ignorance. This is Willful Ignorance, the one who refutes Awareness. Shame is its game, and the house always wins. Ignorance deals out painful memory after memory of losing cards, too many to hold with our so-called frail and trembling fingers. *How did I get these cards, again? Shame, Doubt, Loneliness, Despair. Running out of chips and nothing more to cash in.*

But it's not Real. We don't have to play this rigged game with its fabricated rules.

Mary watches her True Self claiming exactly what Jesus taught right at the beginning of what we have in Mary's Gospel and echoed from the earlier section of the Gospel of Thomas (Saying 77). In Reality, the All comes from Source and returns to Source, in perfect balance and complete harmony.

Let's face it, Perfect Humanity is made for harmony. The connection between the material and Divine happens right here, in our True Nature. No wonder what's called "sin" is that which is contrary to our True Nature. It knocks us out of tune and off rhythm, where there is no resonance.

Contemplative Reflection

How does the True Self's response to Ignorance challenge the notion that judgment and criticism are effective tools for personal growth? What alternative approach does the True Self offer?

This question invites us to consider the limitations of judgment and criticism, and to explore the power of self-awareness, acceptance, and a focus on our inherent connection to Source.

In what ways can the understanding that "everything comes from Source and returns to Source" provide comfort and perspective in the face of challenges and adversity? How can this understanding help us navigate feelings of worthlessness or despair?

This question encourages us to reflect on the cyclical nature of existence and the impermanence of all things. It prompts us to consider how this understanding can offer solace and resilience in difficult times.

Chapter 38 (Pages 16 - 17a)
Confrontation and Revelation

The True Self continued to the fourth level, where the council called Vengeful Anger resided. The group was made of seven figures. The Obscuring, The Craving, and The Ignorance were there, alongside The Deadly Forgetting, The Physical Addiction, The Wisdom of Fools, and The Volatile Violence.

"We have you now. So, murderer, where is it you believe that you come from? And where do you think you were planning to go? You're homeless, a vagrant, there's nowhere you belong, and no one who will ever claim you."

True Self responded, "What has had control over me, what was an oppression, has been killed off. I devoured it and now cannot die."

"Now I'm free from the false pattern, by virtue of the Pattern of the Whole. No longer am I bound by forgetfulness and temporality but move freely in Reality. I am finally—after being filled with wonder and remembering who I am—able to sit with what I've found in this Stillness."

When she had finished sharing, the Tower settled into the Silence. After all, it was from Silence that the Teacher shared with her.

(Standard Translation:
"When the soul had overcome the third power, it went up and saw the fourth power, which took seven forms:

The first form is Darkness; The second, Desire; The third, Ignorance; The fourth, Zeal for Death; The fifth, the Kingdom of the Flesh; The sixth, the Foolish 'Wisdom' of Flesh; The seventh, the 'Wisdom' of Anger.
"These are the seven powers of Wrath.

"They ask the soul, 'Where do you come from, you murderer, and where are you going, conqueror of space?'

"In response the soul said, 'What binds me has been killed, what surrounds me has been overcome, my desire is gone, and ignorance has died. In a [world] I was released from a world, [and] in a type from a type which is above, and from the chain of forgetfulness which exists only for a time. From now on I'll receive the rest of the time of the season of the age in silence.' "

When Mary said these things, she fell silent because the Savior had spoken with her up to this point.)

What This Means

Next level: jewelry, perfume, restrooms? Nope. In fact, those three nasty managers you ran into on the lower levels are all here, along with four more. They must have taken the express elevator.

Some folks link these seven "powers of Wrath" to the "seven demons" Mary had when casually mentioned in Luke's gospel (also added later to Mark). Others go so far as to contrast them with the Seven Deadly Sins and the Seven Virtues, or with the Seven Vials of Judgement in John's Revelation. There's also the Seven Days of Creation, seven notes to music scale... We can get just downright seven-silly! So, let's pull back from projecting just a bit, and let this stand on its own.

I said a bit earlier I would discuss the early Tchacos Codex called The Book of Allogenes (or "Stranger," and quite different from the Nag Hammadi's Allogenes). Here, the Stranger ("not of this world") sounds remarkably like Jesus, accompanied up to Mount Tabor by his disciples.

As Mark Mattison notes:

> "After resisting Satan's temptations, Stranger prays for help. A bright cloud surrounds him, and a voice from the cloud instructs him about his ascent past a number of hostile Powers: Desire; Darkness; Ignorance; Death; the Kingdom of the Flesh; and the Foolish 'Wisdom' of Flesh."

Sounds familiar, huh. Like Jesus revealed to Mary, this was the ancient practice that he used himself. The responses provide a kind of contemplative practice, an examination that led one to "heal" oneself of the "passions" and overcome any "wavering." (Ouch! What a slap to how we see the other students reacting!)

The mantric reply to each oppressing Power, in every climate or level, is always:

> *"Now I'm free from the false pattern, by virtue of the Pattern of the Whole. No*

longer am I bound by forgetfulness and temporality but move freely in Reality. I am finally—after being filled with wonder— able to sit with what I've found in this Stillness."

This is how what *the Teacher* shared plays out. It's in realizing our True Self as a kind of remembering, in letting go of the stuff that's contrary to True Nature, in movement within Awareness. This was demonstrated by the Gospel of Thomas, which begins with the deep seeking, the unsettling, the discovery of wonder, the better understanding of having self-control, and recognition of Presence through Silence.

(See? I told ya it'd keep just unfolding, this concept of "unwavering." And for more on passions and demons, Paulson's work on the Secret Revelation of John does a great job showing how folks in antiquity were hardwired as well to worry about this "evil agitation," and how one learns to overcome it.)

Contemplative Reflection

How does the True Self's journey through the different levels of power and confrontation with the seven powers of Wrath mirror our own internal struggles and challenges on the path to spiritual liberation?

This question encourages us to reflect on our own inner battles with negative emotions, desires, and limiting beliefs. It prompts us to consider how we can navigate these challenges with courage and determination, drawing inspiration from the True Self's unwavering resolve and connection.

What is the significance of the True Self's declaration of freedom from the "false pattern" and the embrace of the "Pattern of the Whole"? How can we align ourselves with this

Pattern of the Whole and break free from the limitations of our conditioned selves?

This question invites us to contemplate the possibility of transcending our conditioned patterns of thought and behavior. It encourages us to seek a deeper connection to our True Nature and to align ourselves with the Consciousness.

Chapter 39 (Page 17b)
Opposition and Betrayal

The student called the Manly One, brother of the Boulder, reacted by turning to the other students and asking, "So what do all of you think of what she's claiming here? I don't know about you, but I can hardly believe the Teacher would say such wildly unorthodox things, so different from everything we grew up with."

The Boulder also chimed in, "That's a great point! There's no way that the Teacher shared anything with a woman but not in front of everyone, especially us. That makes no sense. I wouldn't think he'd expect us to turn around, abandon tradition, and just start following her. And no way would he pick a woman to be our boss!"

(Standard Translation:

In response Andrew said to the brothers (and sisters), 'Say what you will about what she's said, I myself don't believe that the Savior said these things, because these teachings seem like different ideas."

In response Peter spoke out with the same concerns. He asked them concerning the Savior: "He didn't speak with a woman without our knowledge and not publicly with us, did he? Will we turn around and all listen to her? Did he prefer her to us?")

What This Means

Towards the end here, we see an echo from the end of Thomas' gospel—only this time, there's no *Teacher* around to defend *the Tower*, and now the thick-headed student (Peter) has solicited his bully brother (Andrew) to help take her down.

They've missed the point completely. The brothers seem stuck on the first level still. They can't let go of what is "un"Real, and they're unable to move beyond The Obscuring.

Contemplative Reflection

How do the reactions of *the Manly One* and *the Boulder* to *the Tower's* dream and message reflect the challenges of accepting new spiritual leadership, especially when it defies traditional expectations and social norms?

This question encourages reflection on the resistance to change and the ways in which societal conditioning can hinder spiritual growth. It prompts us to examine our own biases and assumptions, and to consider how we might respond to spiritual guidance that challenges our preconceived notions.

Chapter 40 (Pages 18 – 19)
Rebuke, Remember

The Tower was heartbroken, crying, "Boulder? What are you thinking? Do you really believe I would need to make anything up? Why would I lie about the Teacher we all loved and who loved us?"

The student called the Unifying One spoke up, "What are you doing, Boulder? You're always so hasty and hot-tempered. How could you possibly think the right thing to do is to attack a woman—a sister no less and close friend at that—like she's some kind of villainous enemy. It's absurd! We all know the Teacher held the Tower in the highest regard. Exactly who do you think you are to despise and reject her? The Teacher knew her well and trusted her dearly.

"Shame on all of us, we should be embarrassed by our behaviors. So, let's make things right and enter into our Full Humanity, too, living like the Teacher is connected with us still, doing all he taught us."

When the Unifying One finished, everyone dispersed and began sharing what they learned from the Teacher.

(Standard Translation:

Then Mary wept and said to Peter, "My brother Peter, what are you thinking? Do you really think that I thought this up by myself in my heart, or that I'm lying about the Savior?"

In response Levi said to Peter, "Peter, you've always been angry. Now I see you debating with this woman like the adversaries. But if the Savior made her worthy, who are you then to reject her? Surely the Savior knows her very well. That's why he loved her more than us.

"Rather we should be ashamed, clothe ourselves with perfect Humanity, acquire it for ourselves as he instructed us, and preach

the gospel, not laying down any other rule or other law beyond what the Savior said."
When [Levi said these things], they started to go out to teach and to preach.)

What This Means

The Tower has nothing in herself to desire any kind of takeover or to take charge. Since the beginning, she has only sought Oneness. She has learned how it has the vast capacity for caring, healing, and drawing things in. Filled with compassion herself, she lets go and that compassion overflows. She allows the Light to shine brightly from a higher position outside of her physical self alone. This would have been difficult for others to not notice.

The *Unifying One* (Levi/Matthew) defends her.

Traditionally, Matthew was a tax-collector, right? The skills needed to get along with Roman bosses and Jewish taxpayers would have been his to master. This seems to line up with the Gospel of Matthew, too, how it seeks to calm things between Jewish and Gentile Christians.

It's unlikely that he was alone in noticing this aggression and posturing of Peter and Andrew. The account appears to acknowledge that *the Teacher* completely trusted *the Tower*. The rest should have been able to see that he just wanted them all to take what they had learned and share it with everyone.

And that's what we have in the Gospel of Mary.

It's not a bad note to end on, really. It's just the encouragement we need to go and do the same with what we've learned.

Contemplative Reflection

How does *the Unifying One's* call for the disciples to "make things right" and embody *the Teacher's* teachings reflect the ongoing process of integrating spiritual lessons into our daily lives?

This question prompts reflection on the importance of putting spiritual principles into practice, even in the face of internal and external conflict.

What can we learn from the disciples' decision to disperse and share *the Teacher's* teachings? How can we actively participate in the dissemination of spiritual wisdom within our own communities and networks?

This question encourages us to consider our role in carrying on the Teacher's legacy by sharing the teachings and insights we have received. It prompts us to think about how we can contribute to the spread of spiritual awareness in the world.

Conclusion

Now that we've seen how *The Teacher, The Twin, & The Tower* renders this, I hope that you've found something relatable, refreshing, and restorative.

There's little doubt in my mind that each was written to be anti-apocalyptic, maybe even anti-martyrial. Perhaps this is why they resonated with so many early on, after the prophetic efforts were failing following Nero's persecutions and the fall of Jerusalem. Many folks were just trying to survive while holding on to these teachings and would have needed reassurances. They were just as likely a kind of damage control in response to why Jesus had not immediately returned. I believe these themes we see in his teachings may have been why Jesus diverged a bit from John the Baptist—why the message shifts from "The Messiah is coming, and his Kingdom is near" to "The Kingdom is within, and here, now."

This is the full spectrum, high resolution display I've experienced. And personally, I just can't go back to fuzzy shades of gray.

What stands out the most to me with these two gospels is exactly this: there is truly "good news" that embraces all, accentuates all equally, and above all—worth proclaiming!

Acknowledgements

Shirley, I continue to be grateful for all the tireless work you do—and will so much energy and excitement! The blog posts, the podcasts, the classes, the meetings, the reflections throughout the week, it's really something else. I turn to the "Early Christian Texts" (Look it up!) so often. As I've said before, it has all been such nourishment to my soul in this shared journey of exploring the "Bible and Beyond." (This one, too!) I remain forever a fan and friend.

Rachel. You, too, just blow me out of the water with the energy and commitment you've given to making sure anyone has encouragement to dive into the deep waters of apocryphal texts— and to making it freely accessible! Wow! Where would I be without those "Other Gospels" (and *OtherGospels.com* —Ya gotta check that one out, too)!

Sammie, Clo, Jack'son', AJ, (Cozzy & Wan-Wan): You're still my tether that keeps me both from floating off and always aware of which way is up.

Jory, YOU are "All Light!" I'm still enlightened by your insights all the time. What a gift to the world!

Sandy, my friend and editor, you're so skilled and sweet, astute and attuned to the Light. I'm so very grateful for your insights and proofreading prowess!

Bibliography

Bourgeault, Cynthia. *The Meaning of Mary Magdalene: Discovering the Woman at the Heart of Christianity.* Boston, MA: Shambhala Publications, Inc., 2010.

Brock, Ann Graham. *Mary Magdalene, The First Apostle: The Struggle for Authority.* Cambridge, MA: Harvard Theological Studies, 2004.

Butcher, Carmen Acevedo. *The Cloud of Unknowing, With the Book of Privy Counsel.* Boston, MA: Shambhala Publications, Inc. 2009

Cwikla, Anna. "There's Nothing about Mary: The Insignificance of Mary in the Gospel of Thomas 114." *Journal for Interdisciplinary Biblical Studies* 1, no. 1 (2019): 95–112. https://doi.org/10.17613/werw-b083.

De Boer, Esther A. *Mary Magdalene: Beyond the Myth.* San Antonio, TX: Trinity Press International, 1972.

De Boer, Esther A. *The Gospel of Mary: Listening to the Beloved Disciple*. London: Continuum, 2004.

DeConick, April D. *The Original Gospel of Thomas in Translation*. London: T&T Clark, 2007.

Eckhart, Meister. *Selected Writings*. Translated by Oliver Davies. London: Penguin Classics, 1994.

Eliot, T.S. *The Waste Land and Other Poems*. New York: Vintage Classics, 2021.

Falkenberg, René, " What's for Dinner at Salome's Banquet? 'Gospel of Thomas' 61 Revisited," *Annali di storia dell'esegesi 40, no. 1* (2023): 117-139. doi: 10.69071/112233.

Gambhirananda, Swami. *Eight Upanishads, with the Commentary of Sankaracarya, Volume 1*. California: Vedanta Press, 1957

Gathercole, Simon. *The Gospel of Thomas: Introduction and Commentary*. Leiden, the Netherlands: Brill Academic Publishers, 2014.

Guillaumont, A., H. Ch. Puech, G. Quispel, W. Till, and Yassah 'Abd Al Masih. *The*

Gospel According to Thomas. New York: Harper & Row, 1959.

Holmén, Tom and Stanley E. Porter, eds. *Handbook for the Study of the Historical Jesus, Volume 2.* Leiden, the Netherlands: Brill Academic Publishers, 2011.

King, Karen L. *The Gospel of Mary of Magdala: Jesus and the First Woman Apostle.* Santa Rosa: Polebridge Press, 2003.

Koepke, Detlev. *The Jesus of the Gospel of Thomas.* Boston: Metanoia Publications, 2015.

Krosney, Herbert, Marvin Meyer, and Gregor Wurst, "Preliminary Report on New Fragments of Codex Tchacos," *Early Christianity* 1, no. 2 (2010): 282-294. https://doi.org/10.1628/ec-2010-0006.

Leloup, Jean-Yves. *The Gospel of Mary Magdalene.* Rochester, VT: Inner Traditions International, 2002.

Leloup, Jean-Yves. *The Gospel of Thomas: The Gnostic Wisdom of Jesus.* Rochester, VT: Inner Traditions International, 2005.

Linssen, Martijn. "Absolute Thomasine Priority - The Synoptic Problem Solved in the Most Unsatisfactory Manner." *Academia*, (2019a). https://www.academia.edu/40695711/Absolute_Thomasine_priority_the_Synoptic_Problem_solved_in_the_most_unsatisfactory_manner.

Linssen, Martijn. "Two Types of Jesus Parables: Canonical vs. Thomasine, Like Night and Day."*Academia*, (2019b). https://www.academia.edu/40951733/Two_types_of_Jesus_parables_canonical_vs_Thomasine_like_night_and_day. Linssen, Martijn. "The 72 Logia of Thomas and their Canonical Cousins." *Academia*, (2020a). https://www.academia.edu/41668680/The_72_logia_of_Thomas_and_their_canonical_cousins.

Linssen, Martijn. "The True Words of Thomas (Interactive Coptic-English Gospel of Thomas)." *Academia*, (2020b). https://www.academia.edu/42110001/The_true_words_of_Thomas_Interactive_Coptic_English_gospel_of_Thomas.

Linssen, Martijn. "Complete Thomas Commentary, Part I & II (Logion 0-55)." *Academia*, (2021). https://www.academia.edu/46974146/Gospel_of_Thomas_Commentary.

Mattison, Mark M. *The Gospel of Mary: A Fresh Translation and Holistic Approach.* Scotts Valley, CA: CreateSpace Independent Publishing Platform, 2013.

Mattison, Mark M. *The Gospel of Thomas: A New Translation for Spiritual Seekers.* Scotts Valley, CA: CreateSpace Independent Publishing Platform, 2015.

Nikhilananda, Swami. *The Bhagavad Gita.* New Delhi: Prakash Books India Pvt. Ltd., 2023.

Parkhouse, Sarah. *Eschatology and the Saviour: The "Gospel of Mary" Among Early Christian Dialogue Gospels.* Cambridge: Cambridge University Press, 2019.

Paulson, Shirley. *Illuminating the Secret Revelation of John: Catching the Light.* Eugene, OR: Cascade Books, 2022.

Pokorny, Petr. *A Commentary on the Gospel of Thomas: From Interpretations to the Interpreted*. London: Continuum, 2009.

Saxon, Deborah Niederer. *The Care of the Self in Early Christian Texts*. Cham, Switzerland: Palgrave MacMillan, 1997.

Schaberg, Jane. *The Resurrection of Mary Magdalene: Legends, Apocrypha and the Christian Testament*. London: Continuum, 2004.

Teresa of Avila. *The Interior Castle*. Translated by Mirabai Starr. New York City, NY: Riverhead Books. 2004

Watterson, Meggan. *Mary Magdalene Revealed: The First Apostle, Her Feminist Gospel & the Christianity We Haven't Tried Yet*. Carlsbad, CA: Hay House, 2019.

Wolfe, Robert. *The Gospel of Thomas: The Enlightenment Teachings of Jesus*. Ojai, CA: Karina Library, 2010.
Zinner, Samuel. *The Gospel of Thomas: In the Light of Early Jewish, Christian and Islamic Esoteric Trajectories*. London: The Matheson Trust, 2011.

I highly recommend Mark M. Mattison's online offerings of both The Gospel of Thomas as well as The Gospel of Mary (and several other extra–canonical translations) at: www.gospels.net.

His commentaries and footnotes can be found in his books available for purchase.

I would be remiss if I didn't include David Curtis' translation of the Gospel of Mary. It's no surprise such a beautiful piece would come from such a wonderful and creative soul. www.thegospelofmary.org

And if you are looking to explore more early Christian extra-canonical texts, I would eagerly point you in the direction of a continually growing curation, with multiple translations, resources (like Nag Hammadi manuscripts), and even a community link at: www.othergospels.com It's completely free, but I encourage your Patreon support. Paying for translations is not cheap.

About the Author

Toto Tay is an independent researcher, a caregiver and special needs parent, an adoring spouse and "papa bear", a doodle-dad, a wisecrack, an artist, an ally, a friend, and a big, big fan of non-duality in all its forms... and formlessness.